RECOVER[edu]:

A Communication Guide for Addressing Mental Health in Schools

by
Daniel Patterson

Copyright © 2020 Daniel Patterson

All rights reserved. No part of this book may be used or reproduced in any manner whatsoever without prior written consent of the authors, except as provided by the United States of America copyright law.

Published by Best Seller Publishing®, Pasadena, CA
Best Seller Publishing® is a registered trademark
Printed in the United States of America.
ISBN 9798639000713

This publication is designed to provide accurate and authoritative information with regard to the subject matter covered. It is sold with the understanding that the publisher is not engaged in rendering legal, accounting, or other professional advice. If legal advice or other expert assistance is required, the services of a competent professional should be sought. The opinions expressed by the authors in this book are not endorsed by Best Seller Publishing® and are the sole responsibility of the author rendering the opinion.

For more information, please write:
Best Seller Publishing®
253 N. San Gabriel Blvd, Unit B
Pasadena, CA 91107
or call 1(626) 765 9750

Visit us online at: www.BestSellerPublishing.org

Table of Contents

Disclaimer iv
About the Author v
Introduction 1

Section One: The Student's Voice 11
    Chapter One   Intervention and Collaboration 13
    Chapter Two Teacher Autonomy and Accommodations 27

Section Two: The Parent's Voice 41
    Chapter Three What Parents Wish We Knew 43
    Chapter Four Communication and Partnership Strategies 57

Section Three: The Educator's Voice 71
    Chapter Five What Educator's Wish We Knew 73
    Chapter Six What Educators Wish Parents Knew 87

Section Four: The Clinician's Voice 101
    Chapter Seven What Clinicians Wish We Knew 103
    Chapter Eight Levels of Care 113
    Chapter Nine Progressive Programs and Partners 129

Conclusion: Communication Not Isolation 143
Contact 151

Disclaimer

Daniel Patterson is not a licensed medical professional or health care provider. Daniel Patterson is not trained in diagnosing psychological or medical conditions. Daniel Patterson and this book are not substitutes for medical care, psychological care or medical advice. If you require assistance with any mental health or medical issue, please contact your health care provider for any medical care or medical advice. Daniel Patterson makes no guarantees or warranties of any kind, express or implied.

About the Author

Daniel Patterson is the author of the book, *The Assertive Parent* (2018), a roadmap for building autonomy and resilience in teenagers. He has spent over seventeen years in secondary education, serving as an English teacher, tennis coach, student council advisor, and high school assistant principal. He is currently the director of education for a therapeutic high school and runs his own full-time consulting firm, Patterson Perspective Inc.

Patterson has been a featured voice on NBC News, The HuffPost, The Los Angeles Times, Orange County Register, Entrepreneur Magazine, Thrive Global, MSNBC, She Knows, Bustle, and elsewhere. He has been a guest expert on Fox News, TedX, My Dad Pod, The Bruce Cook Show, No Bounds Podcast, Tell Your Story, and Lasting Learning. In addition, he has been a keynote speaker at school, recovery, and parenting conferences.

Having persevered through his own struggles with mental health and addiction, Patterson spends his free time serving on the board of directors of the Imagine Foundation, an organization committed to assisting and empowering struggling young people.

Find him online at:

daniel@pattersonperspective.com
www.pattersonperspective.com
Instagram: @pattersonperspective
Facebook: @pattersonperspectiveinc

Introduction

It's no secret that teenage mental health has reached crisis-level statistics. Teenage suicide rates are climbing, and teens are more stressed out than they've ever been. With the 24-hour news cycle interconnected in real time via social media, students are living in the shadow of school violence in a polarized political system. I could fill these opening pages with graphs, charts, and numbers that illustrate all this, but that information is readily available to anyone who wants it. The question this book proposes is: What can educators and parents do to change the course of these data points?

Each time we lose a celebrity to suicide, for example, the mental health conversation jumps to the front of news cycles and dominates dinner table conversations and social media posts—only to fall back into the abyss days later. To effectively de-stigmatize mental health, we need to talk about it, but instead we talk about talking about it. We have yet to really break down the concepts to make getting help with mental health approachable. Meanwhile, students in the United States and across the globe are struggling with anxiety, depression, sexual identity, disordered eating, video game addiction, porn addiction; and drug, alcohol, and nicotine addiction.

I hear this all the time, especially from teachers of an older generation, "Everybody has anxiety now. When I was a kid, nobody had anxiety." This narrative of plausible deniability is unacceptable; it's not 1985 anymore. It's 2020, and the landscape has changed. Kids today seem to have an easier time talking about it with each other, but they have a harder time talking about it with adults, a feeling that is a direct result of this outdated thinking. In education specifically, students reserve sharing struggles because they fear being judged by their teachers. And parents fear being judged by the adult decision makers within their respective schools or districts.

Students fear that if they admit they are struggling, it may affect playing time on their school team, their potential to earn an A or snag a leadership position, or even their likelihood of receiving the best possible letter of recommendation from teachers. So, it becomes a big secret, and worsens the system. Students keep silent, and their shame and isolation worsens the academic pressure and feelings of anxiety, resulting in an inability to succeed within the confines of the school setting.

With some young people, the symptoms are more obvious, but I've witnessed even high-performing students fall apart. They have the GPA, the test scores, the varsity accolades, and the club leadership roles. From 30,000 feet, they appear high functioning, when in reality, they're crippled with anxiety, depression, or other hidden factors plaguing their vibrancy. They are working so hard "adulting" that they end up turning to substances, or social media, the internet, or gaming as an escape. And eventually the wheels fall off the wagon because they can no longer maintain the work hard, play hard duality of their lives. And the result? They crash and burn; a drop can be sudden and quick.

As educators, we are presented with state standards. Students must be able to do *this* by *this* point. There are benchmark assignments, and benchmark tests they are expected to pass. But where are those benchmarks for mental health? Where are those benchmarks for learning about addiction, or processing trauma?

Even to this day, a van will pull up at a school, and kids will go for their vision or hearing screening. We test for this because we want to know if there's a problem. If they can't see, or they can't hear well, the school wants to address it because it's going to affect their learning. But where's the universal screening for mental health? Where's the universal screening for depression or anxiety?

When I was an assistant principal, the answer I often got to this question was, "If we identify them, then we're responsible for them. And we don't have the resources to deal with the magnitude of what we would find." But by not dealing with it, the problem is only going to get larger. It will reach critical mass. It already has in certain communities, with cluster suicides and anxiety rates climbing. Now I am not suggesting that the obligations solely rest on the shoulders of the education system, but I strongly assert that those in education are best positioned to make a significant impact on our national crisis. If we truly care about students, then we must all act accordingly.

In different leadership positions I've had, resistance to change most often comes from someone claiming, "But we've always done it this way." Well, the way that we have always addressed mental health and addiction isn't working. We need to reshape the way that we approach, how we support, and how we acknowledge students with mental health and substance disorders in our school system.

Intended Audience

RECOVER[edu] strives to take our dialogue about adolescent mental health beyond data and numbers, and into solutions. The goal is to transform the conversation from data drops and cage rattling to one about the tools and information that educators can implement systematically. It's not fair to expect teachers to pick up the weight of the situation without providing them infrastructure, strategies, or connecting them with resources. It's also important to understand why we can't operate on the assumption of outsourcing, or sending kids away. If we want to make a change, we must treat education as an inside job.

Ultimately, kids spend the lion's share of their day in one ecosystem. The group of adults who see kids the most often and most consistently are educators and staff members at their school sites—not their parents, their doctors, their tutors, and so on. If we can layer our educational system and school environments with more safeguards and norms that can better address the daily struggles of our students, we can hopefully prevent further escalation of these markers and trends.

RECOVER[edu] is geared primarily toward educators, and those supporting students. It is intended to encourage educators to better partner with families and to better support students within their own classroom, on their own school site, or within their own district. Granted, much of this book's call to action falls on teachers because they're on the front lines, but the book is intended for anybody who has anything to do with teenagers within the school ecosystem, from support staff all the way to the superintendent of schools.

The larger intended audience includes teachers, counselors, coaches, principals, district officials, support staff, custodians, clerical staff—really anyone who is given the opportunity to shape the day of our students, anywhere in the spectrum, from classroom instruction to greeting them in the attendance office if they're running a few minutes late. This book is also perfect for parents, or anyone in the life of a teenager, looking to better understand how to navigate the educational space when their child is struggling with mental health or addiction.

For additional information beyond the scope of this book, readers can visit my website www.recoveredu.com. On the website you will find a book study to take you through each chapter, as well as additional resources that will be referenced in the related chapters.

Who I Am

I'm writing this book from the perspective of an educator, as well as someone who has struggled with my own mental health and subsequent addiction. This struggle began for me in middle school and ebbed and flowed into my adult years. I consider it very much a miracle that I'm alive today and consider it my God-given purpose to help as many young people as I can. I'm writing this book through the lens of someone who has battled depression, anxiety, and alcohol addiction, but nevertheless, maintained a successful and loving career as an educator.

My career as an educator began teaching sixth grade through twelfth grade. I taught middle school and high school English, and AVID. I was a student council advisor, a varsity tennis coach, and a high school assistant principal. I've taught in low-income schools and high-income schools. I've taught in urban schools and suburban schools. Today, I have my own private consulting firm, Patterson Perspective, Inc., in which I work with students and families across the United States, and even internationally. Additionally, I direct the educational objectives for an alternative day school in Los Angeles for students recovering from mental health disorders and addiction.

In my current roles, I work in close proximity with families struggling, as well as with psychologists, psychiatrists, therapists, and counselors. I believe that this range of experience—as a teacher, coach, administrator, and now as an outside consultant working with clinicians and families—effectively positions me to facilitate shifting the conversation between stakeholders from data and numbers to tangible ideas and solutions.

The Book's Purpose

The primary purpose of *RECOVER[edu]* is to connect the various stakeholders within education and let them know what the others are thinking, or what they need from one another. When I was a teacher, I had little idea what families on the outside of my classroom needed, and when I was an assistant principal, I had very little idea what teachers knew or didn't know about students on their roster. And sometimes, teachers did not have the information essential to keeping our students safe and well within the school setting.

Furthermore, and to no fault of their own, educators often don't fully grasp the totality of resources, channels, and levels of care available to students struggling with mental health disorders and substance abuse. My first book, *The Assertive Parent*, was meant to be a tool guide for parents of teenagers. It dealt with core issues like drugs, alcohol, nicotine, school, academics, technology, social media, and family systems. This book attempts to widen the conversation to include mental health, specifically within education.

Keep in mind that this book isn't just me telling you what to do. In order to bring in the voices of the various stakeholders, I've talked with students, parents, teachers, clinicians and clinical directors, as well as psychiatrists and psychologists. I've included these perspectives so readers can engage in a shared learning experience and a larger dialogue.

On a very primary level, after reading this book, I hope readers will be reminded of some of the common signals of mental health and addiction issues in order to prevent the preventable and treat the treatable. Throughout the book, I will stress the need for clear channels of communication, from support staff all the way up to the superintendent. It should be obvious to an educator who to go to in what situation. If I have a student with X, how do I refer them? What kinds of questions can I ask the parents? How do I better partner with families? What kind of policies can I have in my classroom to make me more approachable?

Other questions this book addresses include:

- How can educators support students who are in various forms of recovery?
- How can educational ecosystems better partner with families dealing with personal crises?
- How can we show up for young people with more presence and fewer assumptions?

I want to empower teachers to feel like they can make informal accommodations for students when necessary. By stretching their own rules, they can become more of a partner to families or students who are suffering from mental health and addiction. We often will bend over backwards for a student with leukemia, cancer, or a rare disease. But with mental health, and especially with addiction, it's often considered a moral defect. So how do we shift this kind of thinking, so we are better prepared to help our students?

Another goal with this book is to encourage educators to examine their own blind spots. For example, I was a very successful educator. I was a high performing professional. I won awards; I earned promotions; I received good press, all while having a significant mental disorder and suffering from addiction. I had no idea how to manage my own mental health, or how to manage my own addiction, and I was leading a classroom and school site. If that's not a good example of a major blind spot, I don't know what is. Because if the leader is suffering in silence and unsure how to triage or manage their own symptoms or life, then how can we expect them to know how to manage that of 100 to 200 students that they have on a roster? To appropriately shift the way mental health is addressed in schools, we must also lead by example.

We must deal with our own personal roadblocks with confidence and tenacity.

It's my observation having worked in education for the last 16 years that mental health disorders and addiction disorders are fairly rampant in the profession. Part of the reason for that is because it's easy to hide. Educators interact primarily with children. We're not in an office setting with other adults reading our body language, temperament, and attitude. Contact with other adults can be a lot like ships passing in the night. We may collaborate occasionally, but generally speaking, we're left to our own devices, and our own system.

This book is intended to begin a larger conversation about changing the way we think about mental health, and the systems we put in place. It should function as a starting point to create a system that works. This book will also address:

- Warning signs that you can look for.
- How and when to communicate your observations and concerns.
- How to have difficult conversations.

Whether you're a teacher, an administrator, school support staff, or a parent, it should prompt you to:

- Determine what you know and what you don't know.
- Figure out what you do well, and what you don't.
- Notice and address your blind spots.
- Clarify what your resources are, or what resources you need but don't have.
- Evaluate our values as a greater society. What are we validating? What are we supporting?

Oftentimes there's an assumption that if students are taking care of business, they can do what they want to do. As long as they have a 4.0 GPA, or they're representing the school positively on the football field or the basketball court—then we can look the other way at their behavior. Instead, I'd like to see a system that focuses less on those shiny markers, and more on the internal makeup of these students that's going to carry beyond school.

We talk about preparing students for life, or preparing them for the next step beyond high school. Well, the next step includes understanding your own mental health, how to have balance, how to respect boundaries, and how to reach out for help if you're suffering. Students need to know that they can do anything, but they can't do everything. They can't have it all and expect to stay healthy and live a long life.

This is why I'm partnering with Patrick's Purpose, a non-profit that I will talk more about in chapter three. Because of the work that they're doing to raise awareness about mental health in the community, I'm donating 10% of the proceeds from this book to them in order to help further this cause that I so wholeheartedly believe in.

So let's begin our conversation.

SECTION ONE

The Student's Voice

What kids with mental health struggles want parents and educators to know.

- The importance of feeling seen, a safe space, and allies.
- Why the current education model could use adjustment.
- The importance of making informal accommodations to support students in recovery mode.

CHAPTER ONE

Intervention and Collaboration

On every school campus, hundreds to thousands of people go through their day in concert with each other—from kids and clerical staff, to teachers and administrators—everyone trying to put their best foot forward. In that organized chaos, it's easy to become isolated as a teacher in your classroom, and isolated as a student. That isolation can lend itself to kids slipping through the cracks, which can be seen by a slow trickle of vibrancy, health, and performance.

Early intervention is key to stopping this. By "early intervention," I'm not talking about grades, or anything academic really. I am talking about the human condition. I'm talking about thriving as a person and feeling confident and well in the school setting from a social/emotional perspective. This is an intangible of grave importance since it dovetails into a healthy learning environment. Early intervention is about restoring order and helping students regain their balance so they can make their way back to social and academic success—whatever "success" looks like to that student in the school setting.

In this chapter, we will examine the importance of communication and connection with respect to early intervention. In short, early intervention is really about crisis avoidance. The word "crisis" can be polarizing because we often think in terms of worst-case scenarios. We focus on the big-ticket crises like a student in an office receiving a threat assessment for suicide ideation. But often, we ignore the micro-crises that slide under the radar, but ultimately become those big-ticket items. The goal is to proactively intervene in these micro-crises. One way to do this is to acknowledge students as individuals, to let them know you see them for who they are. Because a crisis for one student can look very different than a crisis for another.

Early Intervention Saved Me

Part of the reason that I am so impassioned about mental health in high school stems from my own experience and relationship with mental health as a teenager. In high school, I was that student who had a 4.0 GPA and showed well on paper, but I was struggling immensely underneath. In my educational journey, particularly in high school, I felt seen for succeeding in the classroom; I felt seen when elected to student council; I felt seen engaging in community service and getting recognized for those efforts. I also felt seen negatively, as a target for a group of peers who wanted to make my life difficult and remained very committed to that effort. At the time, this was the experience that mattered. My grades and other successes were not indicators of who I was. They were simply boxes I was checking.

I do recall that I had one ally on campus, a woman named Sarah, who was a community liaison, not a counselor. She was a programs coordinator on site through county funding, and she had an office adjacent to the library, which was where I would take refuge from the bullies during lunch breaks and passing periods. Sarah was the one adult who could see that struggle within me. She reached out and offered me support. Without that relationship, I do not think I would have made it through high school.

Sarah's office was always super mellow. She had lamps on, and music. It felt very comfortable and very safe. The first day she invited me in, she didn't ask me, "What's wrong? Tell me all your problems," because she could already see it. It didn't need to be said. That routine of going in there and checking in with her was integral in keeping me moving forward. We would talk about all kinds of things, particularly what the future would look like once I got out of high school. I was able to see a future for myself, when before I felt like I had none.

Everybody needs a Sarah, and it only takes one adult to breathe life or optimism back into a child. Early intervention doesn't have to be formalized. It doesn't have to be systemic or clinical, and it certainly doesn't have to be academic based. It just needs to be human.

Paying it Forward

My experience with Kaley, the first student I maximized my creative problem-solving autonomy for, was informed to some degree by the help I'd received from Sarah. I knew Kaley because I was assistant principal, then, of a seven through twelfth grade school. I'd worked there for a long time and taught her in seventh grade English. Historically, Kaley had good attendance and grades. She was a very successful varsity athlete with intentions to go to a four-year college. Her parents were loving and supportive, but not overbearing. They weren't telling her, "You have to take these classes; you have to go to this college." They wanted to curate her talents and passions.

People rarely come to the assistant principal of a high school to tell them what a great day they're having or how well they did on something. Typically, my role was to help them solve a problem or to deliver a consequence for making a mistake, either behaviorally or academically. One of my tasks each week was to go through the attendance and call anybody into my office with a lot of absences. This week, Kaley was on that list.

The standard operating procedure was to call a student in, talk to them about why they need to come to school, and probably assign a few detentions, which makes no sense to me because they're already not at school, so now they have to be at school extra. But when Kaley arrived at my office and sat across from me at my desk, she was a shell of the person that she had been. So, for the first time, I chose a posture of trying to understand what was making her miss school, rather than focusing on the amount of school she had missed.

That line of questioning set off a domino effect that uncovered a very urgent and severe battle with anxiety. Kaley was barely hanging on, but she had no idea how to get help or what to do. I'd like to take a moment now for Kaley to tell her story in her own words.

Kaley's Story

I first began struggling with anxiety in 8th grade. It caused me to either not be able to attend class, or not be able to sit through a full class without stepping out for a break. In my worst times, I knew my parents always had my back and believed in me when I didn't. However, no matter how much support I had, I always knew deep down that I had to conquer my anxiety on my own. The long-term goal of playing tennis in college helped me keep fighting when it felt impossible to do so.

There were no set directions and standards on how teachers and faculty could help me best, so Mr. Patterson and I worked with my teachers to create a 504 plan. This allowed me to finish out my first semester junior year without failing. The plan included:

- Having take-home exams.
- Being able to take a step out of class without alerting the teacher.
- Getting extensions on assignments.

These accommodations allowed me to still be on the tennis team. After completing my semester, I was transferred to a one-to-one private high school so I could work on my anxiety disorder with the goal of returning to school for my senior year and last season of tennis. My 504 plan also allowed me to take the ACT in a separate room with a proctor, and to take each subject at a separate time. If it were not for the 504 plan, I would not have been able to sit through the ACT in a large room with other students.

This alternative plan did not cure my anxiety. However, it took a lot of weight off my shoulders, so that I could work on myself while being in a "safer" environment. Still being able to play tennis gave me an outlet where I felt no fear.

If you are suffering from anxiety, know that there are so many other students dealing with the same issue. It takes a team to conquer anxiety, so look to your closest friends and family. It helps immensely to know that you are not alone in the journey, and it is hard to start it without support. You are never going to be cured from anxiety, but you can learn how to cope with it. It may seem like it will never get better, but it just takes time.

It's the What, Not the Why

By Kaley's own admission, her struggle with anxiety had been going on for three years before it was outwardly exposed in eleventh grade.

This is a perfect example of why we must layer our daily interactions with students with more methods to identify the slow burns before they turn into a sizeable fire. By acknowledging her as a person, as somebody who was clearly going through something, I stopped short of funneling her through the bureaucracy of consequences and privileges. I was able to identify a critical need and thus change the trajectory of Kaley's last years of high school.

Essentially, I helped connect the parents and Kaley with the teachers and school psychologist. We sat down in one room to lay it all out on the table with transparency. Kaley no longer had to keep her anxiety secret or feel ashamed about it. We assured her we would maintain complete confidentiality within the teaching staff. Now, when she needed to leave a classroom suddenly or when she was not able to be at school, her teachers had a better understanding of the why behind it. Often in education, we get stuck on the infraction and the consequence, rather than the issue behind the behavior.

But this time, we didn't tell her, "You don't fit into our system, and we're going to move you straight out to home hospital or to all alternative education." Instead, we carefully came up with a plan that supported her educational growth, emotional wellness, and recovery. We adjusted her schedule by reducing her day. We allowed her to stay on campus for certain classes in which she felt the most safe and her anxiety was the lowest.

We then coordinated with the school district to have her enroll in independent study courses that she could do on her own at home, or times where she was cognitively well enough to do work, but perhaps emotionally not regulated enough to be in a classroom. Then finally, in a class that she had really done poorly in over time, we allowed her to access a third party educational vendor of a private one-to-one school where she could take classes there, in a one-to-one setting that allowed her to remediate a grade that was very low.

Probably most importantly to Kaley, who was a varsity athlete and a leader on her team—we made sure that tennis wouldn't be taken away from her. Otherwise, a student who was not enrolled full time at a comprehensive school was not eligible to play sports. She would have been robbed of the one thing that she still felt so connected to and that she needed the most at that time.

We were able to do all this for Kaley because collectively, as educators, we decided to ask, "What can we do for Kaley to support her and make this work?" Even though, if I'd looked in the student handbook, all arrows would have pointed to no. No, you can't do that. No, that's not how it works. No, she can't play a sport if she's not here. But instead of focusing on the no, we focused on the new "what." The new what worked really well for her.

Now, in writing this book years later, it wasn't as simple as it sounds. It didn't happen overnight. We took immediate action, and we continued to curate our plan over time, and to adjust it accordingly. The onset of this particular season of her life was during her junior year of high school. And through lots of work and the passing of time, by her senior year of high school she was fully integrated back into the comprehensive setting without any of these accommodations necessary to support her.

One of the roadblocks that I experienced most as the team leader in this was the contrast between how her emotional wellness presented when playing tennis, versus while she was contained in the classroom. For some of her teachers, that was really hard for them to understand. One in particular was seemingly unable to grasp why a student could feel so differently in varying environments.

Understandably, that is an easy trap to fall into. I think the teacher was legitimately trying to understand why Kaley couldn't sit through their class, but could go out and start in a high level, nationally ranked team and succeed. However, the job of the educator is not to understand the why from a clinical perspective. That's not our training. Our job is to help support. It can be helpful to question the why behind student behavior, at least initially, but then we need to focus on the what. WHAT can we do? This is the question to ask, rather than getting fixated on the why.

What Students Wish Educators Knew

For the last four years, I've been working in the capacity of an educational-centered coach. That means that I work one-to-one with a student, typically a high school student, and also with that student's parents. We might work on time management, stress management, college applications, job placement or internships, family communication, or teacher communication. I might also help triage school discipline or advocate for students to have accommodations or other support in the school setting.

I feel very blessed to have worked closely with hundreds of students and their families, each with their unique needs. It has also provided me a unique opportunity to see education from the other side of the fence. For the first 14 years that I was involved in education, I was on the school side, and from that perspective I had a hard time understanding the point of view of the family.

Now, on this side of the fence, having worked with so many different kids, regardless of their background, the specific reason that they're in my office, or the specific objectives or goals that we're working towards— I've discovered that at the end of the day, most of them have very similar needs. Despite their differences, their core needs and what they wish educators knew are very congruent with one another.

Importance of a Safe Space or Ally

Similar to my experience with Sarah and the experience that I was able to then pay forward to Kaley, many of the students I know simply don't feel like there's an identifiable adult on their campus that represents a safe space or an ally. The barrier of policies, rules, and other roadblocks that have been created over time result in students feeling like they can't communicate openly. These barriers can be infrastructure-related, with guidance counselors having large caseloads and limited availability; others can be cultural, wherein the competitive spirit among peers leaves little to no room for students to express vulnerability.

In elementary schools, the "buddy bench" concept has gained traction as a tangible mechanism for students to express their feelings of isolation or exclusion. Brightly painted buddy benches are defined safe spaces for students, and when they are utilized, other stakeholders—

such as peers or adult educators—engage with the student to address their needs. But where is the teenage version of the buddy bench for middle and high school students? And how do we as educators curate a method to make the unseen feel validated?

Students Want to Be Seen

If I could identify just one desire for high school students and middle school students in the school setting, it's that they want to be seen. My experience in the classroom, as an assistant principal, and now with families tells me that certain student behaviors are big flashing lights. The following signals may indicate to the adults in their life that they don't feel seen:

- Refusing to attend school.
- Using drugs or alcohol.
- Being very oppositional or disrespectful.
- Breaking the rules.

Obviously, this is not a new concept. But, when students are struggling with social problems, issues at home, or feeling inadequate within the academic reality of their days, they tend to send flares into the sky in the form of misbehavior; and those misbehaviors tend to escalate as they seek to catch somebody's attention.

As an assistant principal, I had to give a lot of bad news and issue a lot of discipline or consequences—whichever you prefer to call it. So it's always a nice surprise to learn that the way I approached something differently, or the way that I both issued a consequence and made a student feel seen simultaneously had a real impact.

Not that long ago, a former student at the school where I was the assistant principal, sent me a message on Instagram. She had posted about graduating from college, and I made a positive comment congratulating her. She then DM-ed me. She said, "Do you remember when I was in your office, and you told me that you understood I was different from the other kids at the school, and how you encouraged me to pursue a path that was non-traditional?" I did remember. She was sitting in my office crying because she hated school and refused to show up.

Instead of pursuing a four-year degree, she went to fashion school in Los Angeles, and now she has a thriving career. Rather than trying to force her in the box of a typical peer or a college-ready peer, I saw her for who she was. That validation from an adult was all she needed. Then, not only did she do better in school and come to school more regularly, she ended up pursuing her core passion.

The Current Education Model Needs to Go

To go back to Kaley's example, she didn't know specifically what she needed or what she wanted. But we were able to arrive at a tangible plan that we could execute, one in which she was granted autonomy and grace in how she navigated her school day. Many of the students that I work with feel similarly as Kaley and the student from the previous example. They see the current schooling model, with that inflexible bell schedule and limited class offerings with a fast track to college, as outdated and irrelevant.

I work with many kids who are motivated from within to go to college, rather than through externally applied pressure. But many I work with simply feel trapped, or like they're chasing a college dream that is not their own.

When I was in high school—and my experience is very traditional—going to college equated to a certain level of financial independence and career success. But our kids are exposed to so many more options and opportunities now. The landscape really has changed. It used to be that a student didn't have to pursue a post-secondary track that would take them to a four-year college. They could still earn a good living, including benefits and a retirement, with the traditional trades like plumber, mechanic, or electrician. Well, it turns out, they still can! But somehow this messaging has become lost and considered less viable.

Yet those trades are still more palatable for parents, and educators oftentimes, as an acceptable trade off to a four-year degree. But we have a whole genre of next generation careers that are blossoming right now in the tech space, with video games, social media influencing, and video sites like Tik-Tok and YouTube.

Now, I'm not saying to everyone that comes into my office, "Yeah, you should be the next YouTube rapper. Get a face tattoo and call it a day." But I am saying that the traditional algorithm as we know it in school feels very outdated. Students then feel disenfranchised, and as a result they become robots going through their day void of passion, interest, and any hope that what they're doing is going to lead them to something that will fulfill them in the long run.

As an example of this systemic bureaucracy that I'm referencing, take the fact that a standard course offering sheet has very few electives outside of art or a world language. Yet a student is typically stonewalled if they are interested in taking a class at a community college, online, or anywhere outside the typical school day. Many school systems don't have avenues in place for students to do this, so students are forced to stay in line and move through the system accordingly.

Some school districts have gotten better at partnering with local community colleges and offer dual enrollment programs, where students can earn high school and college credit at the same time. However, usually only one or two pre-determined courses are offered and set by the school. And these courses are often aligned with the same typical business-focused path that does not pair with the students' passions. Schools say that they are interested in kids extending their learning and having outside experiences, but with most there is no protocol in place for a student to access that opportunity.

Conclusion

I shared Kaley's story as a reminder that if you are a school leader, you are also a decision maker on a school campus. You have authority, and you have a fair amount of autonomy to find loopholes, look for gray areas, or even bend rules slightly. You can implement emergency, or unofficial, accommodations for a student in order to provide them with respite and room to heal, while not robbing them of the experience of being at a comprehensive school. Kaley's story is also one of crisis avoidance. We know that her anxieties had been building for four years before they garnered the attention of the school, and I hate to think of the end result had the school not intervened. It also makes me wonder how many other students are currently in that slow burn state, waiting for someone to meet their needs.

As illustrated in Kaley's story, there's undeniable truth in the fact that when educators communicate, coordinate, and collaborate with families, then positive change can occur. Sometimes that means thinking outside the box or looking for gray areas. It could mean getting informal accommodations. It could mean reexamining the rules, policies, and procedures that have previously dictated decision-making.

It is essential to look at all this with a fresh set of eyes and to become more familiar with ownership, autonomy, and authority as an educator. Only then can we make the best decisions in the interest of students and their health. Again, I'm not talking about every child in every situation—and I am starkly aware of the difference between a bad day or irresponsibility, and a student with clinically-driven needs. When you are granted the gift of identifying a critical need of a student who is struggling immensely, I hope you will look at that as an opportunity rather than an obligation. I hope you will see it as a chance to positively impact their future and problem solve. I hope you will use collaborative skills to make a difference in that child's life.

And as to my own bullies from middle and high school, I now owe them a thank you. It was that constant exposure to very aggressive efforts by peers—and the fact that few adults in my life seemed willing to see what I was really going through— that made me committed to a life of education, but also to doing it differently. I have tried to live each day, and teach each day, and principal each day, so that maybe, just maybe, another student won't have to go through what I went through. In this way, maybe I can change the trajectory of their future.

In the next chapter, we'll look at ways to collaborate and problem solve to better support students, with a focus on fostering teachers' autonomy to grant informal accommodations. In the meantime, please visit www.recoveredu.com for the book study, supplement resources, and relevant links that accompany the content of this chapter.

CHAPTER TWO

Teacher Autonomy and Accommodations

The typical landscape of a middle school or a high school is embedded with markers, standards, and other goal posts for a typical student. These keep the day moving, keep kids safe, and keep everyone, for lack of a better term, "in check." But when we are talking about students who are suffering from a mental health disorder, recovering from addiction, or actively battling either of those two—it's very important that educators and educational systems approach the matter as more of a team sport in terms of lending support and being flexible and accommodating where they can. We're all familiar with formal accommodation, like an IEP plan or a 504 plan. But more often than not, what kids in these circumstances need are unofficial accommodations.

This chapter is geared toward classroom teachers as well as school leaders and decision makers who can empower teachers to feel confident and comfortable making exceptions to rules in order to support students who are in a recovery mode. These leaders may be department chairs, school administrators, curricular leaders, or even district administrators who provide thresholds and autonomy for sites to make changes at their school.

For classroom teachers, I want to make it clear up front that I'm not trying to tell you that you need to do these kinds of accommodations, or have this threshold of variance for every student. I'm talking only about those students with the most critical need. These are students like Kaley in the previous chapter, who are dealing with issues that affect their ability to perform at the same level as someone who is not going through the same struggles that they are. Yet at the same time they would benefit greatly from staying in school, in a typical classroom with typical peers.

Partnering with Parents and Students

In my role as an administrator at an alternative high school for students in recovery from mental health and drug or alcohol addiction, I often see parents who don't want to share information. They're very hesitant to release information to specific teachers or school sites for fear of being judged. They don't want a diagnosis to negatively impact educational access for their child. Often, families operate within a shame and fear mentality. This is because, quite simply, they haven't received assurance from their educators that sharing information is okay, necessary, and will not impact them negatively. And while many educators would never intentionally cause harm, that assurance needs to be communicated loud and clear.

Students are also particularly uncomfortable sharing their reality with teachers, particularly when those teachers traditionally operate a no-exception operation. One simple strategy for teachers to open lines of communication is to be up front about the fact that exceptions can and will be made in times of critical need. They can include language to this effect on their website, in their syllabus, when speaking to students, and when meeting parents at back-to-school night. Really, all of the above is best.

Informal wording can be something like, "Hey, if you are going through something, or if your child is going through something, and it's confidential, you can come to me. I will partner with you, and I will work with you. These rules are the baseline, but exceptions can be made with transparent communication."

A statement of affirmation, or a statement of partnership can move mountains with students in recovery. When I was a teacher, I would partner with anyone, but few were communicative enough to access that partnership fully. I wanted my students to be successful, and I know you do as well. Educators are inherently passionate about kids. We want to help them, but it's easy to become lost in rules, deadlines, and stacks of papers to grade. It's easy to overlook the fear, shame, and the uncertainty that families are dealing with. So fortifying your efforts to initiate the conversation is imperative.

I've noticed frequently that when a specific teacher has reached out like that, it changes the entire dynamic. The student is much more trusting and motivated to try to get what they can done for that teacher because they feel understood rather than alienated.

What Students Wish Adults Knew

As an educator, it's easy to see very obvious signs of mental health issues and obvious signs of addiction. Sometimes these signs look exactly how you imagine they would. But for so many of our kids, they are far less obvious.

One of the biggest lessons that I've learned from being in education, first as a classroom teacher, then as an assistant principal, and now as the director of an alternative high school—is that the idea I had in my mind of what a student might look like, act like, or be like when they were struggling was very different from those markers in reality.

A great majority of students who were struggling the most with addiction or mental health were able to keep up a façade of a typical, healthy, functional student for a long time. Varsity athletes like Kaley, with strong grade point averages who tested high on standardized tests, like the ACT or the PSAT. They were in school leadership groups, and they had lots of friends. If one were to solely evaluate based on their resumes you would never assume that those kinds of kids were struggling.

We also tend to miss kids in that middle percentage, those who aren't the high performers but also not at the lowest threshold, so they don't personify the red flags that typically garner attention. We often fail to meet their needs, which contributes to more stress, anxiety, depression, and substance use in our schools.

Behavior is Tied to Struggle/Recovery

There were several things that I discovered these students wished the adults in their life knew. First, the manifestations that these kids exhibit are directly related to the recovery process that they are in. For example, it may be difficult for these students to:

- Make it to school on time.
- Show up to school at all.
- Complete an assignment on time.
- Concentrate for an extended period of time on a test.

And these factors have nothing to do with intrinsic motivation or their desire to do well in school. In fact, students repeatedly tell me that they want nothing more than to be successful. They wish that they had the energy. They wish they had the ability, cognitively and emotionally, to carry on the activities, complete the assignments, and go through the motions that their friends do so easily. They wish beyond measure that they were just like their peers.

It's easy for adults to misinterpret these behaviors as simple defiance, or to take it that they simply don't care or have no desire to go to college. They may even come across as entitled. However, these behaviors are much more complicated. These manifestations foster negative relationships with teachers and parents leading to further frustration, isolation, and suffering.

Rules Can be Suffocating

As a teacher, I attempted to maintain policies that were straightforward and transparent. For example, if you turn this assignment in late, it's this percent off. Or after this many days, you can't turn it in. Or there are no retakes if you miss the day of the test, etc. For the general school population, this is acceptable, but for those in critical states of need, it is far from effective.

Students struggling with mental health or in the recovery process often have time-consuming obligations beyond the school day. They likely have individual therapy, group therapy, and may be on medication that affects energy levels. Even if they're not on an official support plan, it's critical that the school culture is one where the students feel supported.

When teachers have ironclad policies that don't bend without formal accommodations in place, we really do a disservice to these kids. They continue to lose trust in adults, which is counterproductive to moving through the recovery process. My experience has shown me that students who are suffering from even low-grade struggles tend to get worse before they get better when faced with negative reactions by adults. This includes stonewalling, as well as simply not getting the help that they need. Prioritizing rules over a student's struggle upholds a culture that views mental health and substance abuse as a character flaw or moral deficiency, as opposed to the health issue that it is.

Words vs. Actions

Both as an assistant principal and as a teacher, I've heard many people make statements about understanding students' struggles with mental health. But I've only rarely seen that understanding converted into an actionable, tangible system, either within the classroom or the greater school community.

We talk a lot about talking about mental health, like I stated earlier. We have awareness campaigns on school campuses, and we post suicide hotline numbers that students can text if they're feeling low. We do generalized things like that. But on the daily human level of the adult in the classroom and students in seats, how are you demonstrating empathy and compassion? If you are waiting for an official diagnosis or an official accommodation to come across your desk before you give grace and start to form a relationship, oftentimes it can be too late.

I'd like to reiterate that I'm not talking about just any student. You would not be giving everyone in your classroom unlimited chances to do anything. I'm talking about only those students whose parent, counselor, or doctor has shared information with you. Because you know something is happening, you have that ability as an educator to sidestep your own syllabus.

I know a lot of teachers fear, and I would too, when I was teaching: "If I make this exception for you, then I have to make this exception for everyone." But you're not setting a new bar. In the case of mental health and recovery, the students you are supporting are unlikely to spread the word of any exceptions you've made for them. Remember, they want nothing more than to be like the typical peers in their classroom.

In chapter seven, we'll go into the clinician's perspective and detail what different programs might look like for students. But to give you some idea here, when a student is suffering from a mental health disorder and they are enrolled in an Intensive Outpatient Program (IOP), they would be required to have group or individual therapy after school, typically for at least three hours, maybe three to five days a week.

So, in addition to going through their school day, they have significant obligations that are often life or death critical to their health. They don't have the option not to do them. They might also be taking medication, or the recovery and therapy process might be so draining that they're not able to complete assignments or to be prepared for a test on the specific day it's given.

As such, the degree that you care about their health is defined by your ability to convert that claim into a tangible plan for that student. You can allow them extra time, or perhaps only assign essential standards. Rather than assigning the 50 questions you do for others, you can assign the 20 most essential ones instead, thereby extending grace and capturing your data points simultaneously. You don't need to make them jump through the same hoop of accountability as you would a healthy, typical peer because their realities are very different.

Hybrid Models that Support Students

This section is very much for our school leaders, again, as you are the decision makers in this capacity. There are many different variances to that IOP process I mentioned in the previous section. A student's outside needs, clinical needs, or recovery needs can be vast. As a school leader, it's important to carve out opportunities for students to obtain their education while also working on their health.

Oftentimes we exist in an either/or environment. Either you can be here with us at school doing it our way, or we're going to outsource you to this independent study program or this treatment center. But the goal should always be to make it work in your own ZIP code. These students want nothing more than to be healthy, and it can feel like a punishment when you essentially say to them, "We're so inflexible that if you cannot fit into this box of how we do things in this school environment, you have to be all the way out."

One way to be more flexible is to allow students to take a class that's not offered at your high school. Students in recovery are highly motivated by online or community college courses that connect to their intellectual passions. So rather than taking a standard class on campus, they would take the alternative course, which is very important in the recovery process because it points them toward future thinking about college and beyond. Additionally, it also provides flexibility in their day for therapy and treatment needs.

Reduced days are also important. Most school districts have an independent study element or offering, which allows them this. And oftentimes these are reserved for our home hospital students, those who are critically ill and cannot be on the school campus. Again, mental health and substance recovery is treated different because it doesn't bleed. You don't see it. You don't put a cast on it. Unfortunately, since it doesn't look like other illnesses, there is a tendency not to treat it as such, even though ethically we must.

Independent study options are beneficial for students in recovery, but they can become, again, an either/or situation. Either you can be on campus, or you can do independent study. Now, independent study can also be very isolative since there is no peer interaction. For this reason, it is not always recommended for students in these situations. However, offering a hybrid schedule can be a viable option. Perhaps a student takes two or three classes on campus to maintain a footprint socially, while also doing a reduced day with independent study.

Restorative Justice

Restorative justice can really benefit students in middle schools and high schools. The model recognizes that student behaviors are results of other factors. For example, if a student is coming to school high, there is a core reason. Perhaps they are suffering from addiction, abuse, or neglect. Maybe they're being enabled by negative peers or by any variety of factors. Critics bemoan the model as one lacking accountability. However, effective restorative justice doesn't give permission for anyone to come to school high. What restorative justice says is that when you make that negative choice, or resort to negative coping skills, we're going to provide you with support and high accountability. Traditionally we ask students have high accountability void of support. High accountability minus support, in California at least, looks like disallowing students to make up missed schoolwork from a suspension. So not only do they miss school, they also miss the opportunity to learn. Their grades fall, they grow more disenfranchised, and their behaviors worsen.

As an example, take a student who is caught with marijuana on campus or comes drunk to a school dance or a school game. School policy might tell you to suspend them. But if they're sitting at home suspended for three to five days, they may just be using more. They also have not learned anything other than if they use substances, they get out of school. In that instance, we're not providing the student with any support, just accountability.

Again, restorative justice is about high support, high accountability. We're still going to tell them that they can't drink or do drugs at school. We're still going to tell them to be accountable for their actions. But we're going to offer them an alternative to that traditional consequence or punishment, and hopefully provide education on the matter. We'll keep them in the school day, although obviously not if they are intoxicated at that moment, and apply accountability within the framework of support and learning.

For accountability, perhaps it's community service or a class on addiction. Perhaps it's volunteering somewhere locally, or helping a special education teacher in their classroom—anything to help them feel connected while reinforcing that if they use, they won't be rewarded with isolation. Restorative justice can be creative, innovative, progressive, and community-driven. It can also be a powerful way to learn from a mistake and build positive coping skills.

Unofficial or Informal Accommodations

Ultimately, most of our critical students suffering from mental health or addiction will receive formal accommodation. But the ones at the level just below that threshold may not. For this reason, as an administrator, I recommend educating the staff on the concepts of empathy, compassion, and grace.

I would also provide tangible examples. If I'm a new teacher and somebody tells me, "You can give an unofficial accommodation," I might have learned about that in my credentialing program, but I've never actually put that into practice; I don't know what that looks like. Provide examples, and empower teachers to take that extra step. Amplify this, not only verbally, but in print as part of the new teacher or staff handbook. Make it clear to staff that they are allowed supportive autonomy.

Again, I understand the threshold of official accommodations. But if you've ever experienced the process of obtaining accommodations, it can be several months in the making. Let's say it takes three months, which is most of a semester, to obtain official accommodations. Now imagine if within that window teachers are not willing to provide unofficial accommodations. That student very likely will end that three-month period with failing grades.

Once failing, students avoid school. Attendance plummets. And it creates the perfect storm. To avoid this, we should be flexible with these students while official accommodations are procured. Or even with those in temporary turmoil who don't or won't qualify for long-term official accommodations.

Accommodation Roadblocks

Teachers can face hurdles with granting unofficial accommodations when collaborating on teams. For instance, if you have a group of five teachers and they all teach tenth-grade English, the goal is to have curricular alignment. This means reading the same novels and teaching the same concepts at the same time. They have the same benchmarks, assignments, and so on.

On that team, you might have a strong-willed veteran teacher with outdated viewpoints toward mental health. You may also have a new teacher fresh out of the teacher education program, very willing to support students in more progressive ways. The politics of a curricular team can get messy in ways harmful to students when the less-experienced teachers are then afraid to operate outside of the unspoken rules of that curricular team.

School leaders can address such issues by talking to their department chairs or the entire team. They can make it very well known that when we have a student with a diagnosis, or with a critical situation at home, that individual teachers may modify assignments, timelines, or testing protocols while maintaining the integrity of the school and also supporting student needs.

Extracurricular Activities

When students are suffering, they often have a hard time with work completion or even attendance stemming from factors previously mentioned. But they still want to play their sport, like Kaley, or they still want to be in the theater or dance program. And therapeutically, motivationally, and intrinsically, these activities are vital to them.

But those extracurriculars are often taken away if a student is not at full-time enrollment at that high school, or if they're not meeting specific attendance thresholds. And again, I agree with those policies for a typical peer.

But when our students are going through a treatment process, a recovery process, or are having a particularly hard time with their mental health—it's those extracurricular activities that provide peer interaction, and the optimism and hope that keeps them moving forward. It's this motion we need to encourage as we help fortify their coping skills, so they can reach the other side of the bridge they're crossing.

In the work that I do now, I'm frequently negotiating and facilitating remote work completion. Sometimes I find that schools don't want to partner. I may have a middle or high school student at a facility receiving treatment for mental health or substance abuse, and the school doesn't really want anything to do with it. They may even tell families to un-enroll from the school.

The metaphor that I've used with administrators and district officials successfully is, "Would you be acting this way with the family if that student was at a hospital receiving chemotherapy and treatment for leukemia?" And that goes back to our frame of looking at mental health and substance abuse as a character flaw or a moral deficiency. We're not treating it medically. And again, if you say you understand, and you say you care, then you need to activate policies that match your language.

Accommodations as a Step-up and on Re-entry

In my role now, I work to establish accommodations as a step-up. This means keeping students in the comprehensive school setting, within the typical school model, with layers of accommodations to support them. The goal is always to keep students in the least-restrictive environment.

And let's say despite those accommodations, we reach a tipping point where the student must exit the school setting and go to a higher-level care and receive treatment somewhere else. Hypothetically, they're gone for six months by the time that they've exited and stabilized and been treated, and now they're going to return.

The transition home can often be more difficult than the exit out. But people who might not be familiar with that process might assume, "Well, they've gone, they've received treatment, they're well now." Kind of like, "You have a fever; now it's gone. So now you're back, and I don't have to treat you like you have a fever." But many of those students are going to have a significant adjustment period where they're getting used to being back into motion, back into a multi-period day, back to having multiple teachers, and back to juggling lots of assignments and extracurriculars.

So the accommodations provide a safety net to help soften the landing. The goal is to help integrate them back into the flow of their normal life without becoming overwhelmed and reverting to old behaviors or medical conditions from which they worked to free themselves.

Conclusion

A school system can't operate and will not flourish without structure, boundaries, and safeguards for our students. But if you are in active communication with the family, their counselor, or you otherwise have specific information that something is going on with them, then I believe it's a moral obligation to act even if you don't have the safeguard of a formal accommodation.

The partnership between schools and families starts at the top. The site administrator sets the tone for the department chairs, the team leaders, and all the teachers. They do that with the policies in their staff handbook, in-services, trainings, and the support that they offer. And they do that by supporting teachers when they change their daily practice to benefit students in real-time, as needed.

As a teacher, you can set the tone with headings on your website, syllabus, and classroom decor, like, "How to communicate with me." Or, "How to problem solve through an assignment if you reach a personal obstacle." When families feel that you are open to partnering, and you partner with them, even slightly, it will change the chemistry of the entire relationship. They're going to share more with you on a human level. And from that, you can make more compassionate decisions about how to help them navigate those critical times.

What I've discovered is that as counterintuitive as it is, the specifics of education, like core concepts, timelines, due dates, and credits earned, all have to be put to the side temporarily. They must be secondary to the pure human element of mental health and recovery. Because when students feel marginalized, as if their struggle doesn't matter enough for a teacher or a school to act in their favor, then that can lead to complete disenfranchisement from the school setting. It can lead to dropping out of high school or elevating negative behaviors to critical, and sometimes fatal, levels.

Like Kaley's story from the previous chapter demonstrates, a lot of these matters don't go on forever. With the correct clinical care and accommodations, students can be brought back to a baseline. They can find success again. And what they've learned is, "Hey, I reached out to an adult. That adult listened to me. That teacher listened to me. That authority figure heard me. They worked with me. And I now have a positive relationship with authority figures. I have a positive relationship with my teachers. And I can trust them." Then, the next time they run into a roadblock, they will be less likely to keep it a secret.

Our next chapter is more aligned with the parents' perspective and deals with the sensitive topic of teenage suicide. What are the things that parents who have experienced such a tragedy want the rest of us to know? It will explore how can we better partner with parents to help prevent tragedies. In the meantime, please visit www.recoveredu.com for the book study, supplement resources, and relevant links that accompany the content of this chapter.

SECTION TWO

The Parent's Voice

What parents of kids with mental health struggles want educators to know.

- Signs parents wish educators would look for.
- The importance of programs like Patrick's Purpose and Challenge Success in changing toxic school culture.
- What parents in crisis want from the school community.
- Strategies for clear communication and partnering with parents.

CHAPTER THREE

What Parents Wish We Knew

Our teenagers exist in a school-wide, community-wide, system of education and obligation. Many are taking advanced classes and trying to increase their test scores. In athletics, they're being pushed to make varsity or pursue that college scholarship. Maybe they're dancing several hours a day to try to make a team, or they're trying out for a part in the next school show.

Either way, our kids are overextended. But they don't want to disappoint their parents with low grades. They don't want to disappoint their teachers by not taking a higher-level class. They don't want to disappoint their college counselor by not completing their 50+ hours of community service.

All of this equates to chasing the college carrot, and the idea that a college education at a certain school will guarantee success. In order to reach it, they must do x, y, and z and work, work, work, work. But many cannot handle the pace, and they're exhausted, struggling with mental health, relying on nicotine, and abusing drugs or alcohol. They may even think to themselves, "I can't do these things. Because I can't do these things, I will never attain success as it's defined for me. Therefore, I have no way out."

That's when our kids make really bad decisions. This chapter addresses sensitive material: Specifically, teenage suicide. Suicide is the second leading cause of death for teenagers in America. When students reach the point where they want to take their own life, it's important to look at what we can do at the school level, as well as a greater community, to intervene.

This chapter is much more attuned to the parents' perspective, and it addresses the adult communication between parents and the school community. A school community includes any adult in the spectrum of the school, including coaches, teachers, principals, counselors, tutors, or anyone who has any role, formal or informal, helping a child get through their school day.

Patrick's Story

Patrick is an example of a child essentially operating in two synchronous worlds without any overlap in terms of communication. In other words, the signs that his parents had noticed only in retrospect, they obviously hadn't communicated. What was discovered later were some of the issues that Patrick was experiencing at school, such as frustration with his courses and teachers, as well as the amount of rigor and social pressure being placed on him.

While Patrick had voiced his discontent with certain classes to the teachers, those teachers had not communicated this to the parents; his feelings had been marginalized and pushed aside. And Patrick had never taken his concerns and elevated them to a counselor or administrator. There was a void in communication whereupon Patrick's concerns with the school didn't get home, Patrick's parent's concern came only in retrospect, and we ended with a tragedy.

I've brought in Patrick's parents throughout this chapter to share their perspectives on their son and what happened. Here is a description of Patrick, in his dad's words.

Patty was always "all in" whatever it was. Whether skiing the hardest run, cooking a five-egg breakfast, or sleeping, he did it big and

> with everything he had. He loved the outdoors. He could spend all day on a ski mountain (always wanting to catch the last lift of the day), at the beach body surfing, or on the river doing every water sport imaginable. He was also the best of the family at every activity but was always humble about his prowess.
>
> He loved to play football and baseball, but he loved practice even more than the games because he loved to just play and hangout with his friends. He loved competing, but he didn't like competing with his teammates. He hated to see kids not playing or being left out.
>
> He was also the epitome of "cool." He had his own style like wearing mismatched socks and loved his big head of hair, or as we called it "the flow." Patty was good at school but it was not his passion. Kim and I always said he was going to be a fishing guide in the summer and a ski patrol in the winter.
>
> He loved his family. He never left the house without saying, "I Love You." He and Emily loved Go Pro'ing all of their activities, especially at the beach. With James at college they would talk after every game, going over virtually every play. Brandel was his roommate, drove him to school every day, and was his personal catcher. I think Brandel said in his eulogy, "He was my Patrick, and I was his SpongeBob."

As his dad's description above illustrates, Patrick was actively and lovingly participating in his family system at home with his mom, dad, and three siblings. He was not exhibiting isolative behavior or severe aggression. Still, Patrick took his life. It was just before final exams, and a month beyond his sixteenth birthday. Obviously, it was very unexpected. His parents classify it even to this day as Patrick making a very bad mistake that he couldn't take back.

Patrick was not overly outgoing. He seemed confident socially, but he was very disenfranchised from the school perspective. Patrick wrote several letters to his family and to the school community outlining why he made the choice that he did. Essentially, while he had good grades, he felt dominated by the environmental pressures of being at school, under the culture of competition and the pursuit of perfection. He felt isolated, even though he was surrounded by people every day.

Patrick felt like he was being tracked through a system of comparison and data points rather than being rewarded for any individual qualities, like kindness. From his perspective, the only attributes that mattered were markers like grades, how many friends you had, and what level you were on. It was rarely about human connection or being a good person.

Patrick's mother adds, "He had many friends at school, and we learned so many beautiful stories after his passing about what a kind and generous person he was to kids who were new to the school or felt left out. He was never bullied and was admired by his peers for his kindness, humor, and inclusivity. Everyone seemed to be shocked that he took such a drastic measure."

What Parents Want Us to Know

Parents want educators to know, and I do too—that mental health, specifically suicide, can be preventable when the signs are caught. Mental health conditions are treatable. They don't have to lead to suicide.

According to Patrick's mom, "Our public schools must recognize that teen mental health is a huge issue. Social media, gaming, internet access, academic pressure, and parent pressure are all factors that affect teen mental health. Educators must get on board to recognize students who are struggling and to provide effective resources to support families and students. Bringing speakers and programs to campuses to address these issues will support students, parents and educators."

If we can recognize students who are struggling, as Patrick's mother urges, then we can catch them by changing the way that we communicate. As educators, where are our blind spots? Where do we not have connectivity between the different looks that our kids give? Where are students' feelings being disregarded?

Connect to Catch

In order for us to make changes systemically we have to embrace the mindset that teenage mental health is a team sport. There's nothing more important than defining, clearing out, and maintaining channels of communication so that we can check and cross reference different ways that people see students throughout their day. From the time they wake up, to the time that they go to bed.

The theory that I'd like to introduce here is what I call "connect to catch." Essentially, by connecting the different adults in the spectrum of a kid's life, we can compare their different environments and the different looks that we get from that child. The aim is to decrease the school to home divide. A "look" is how a student acts, performs, or behaves in a specific setting. Whereas they may appear vibrant in one setting, like athletics, they may be extremely lonely, sad, isolated or frustrated in a specific academic class, at lunch, in the library, etc.

Our students have unique relationships with everyone in their life. They're going to have a specific relationship with their parents. They're going to have specific relationships to peers and teachers in different classrooms. They're going to act differently on the playground, or at lunch, or in passing period. They may conduct themselves a certain way on the athletic field, or in rehearsals for the performing arts. It is imperative that you assume you are the only one in their life that may be seeing a warning sign, or who suspects that all is not well. If you have a concern, immediately cross check that observation with their other adult constants.

Each of the adults in a teenager's life will have a unique vantage point and must communicate with each other, or check in, so that they can compare notes. Of course, this is keeping in mind that a student might act one way in the classroom, another way at home, and another way on the field. Sometimes, by not communicating, or assuming others will report concerns, we miss very crucial tell-tale signs that things are not well with a student, and that they need help.

Signs Parents Wish Educators Would Look For

In speaking with Patrick's parents, I asked them if there were signs in retrospect that they felt that they missed. That's a hard question to ask parents, and certainly it was brave of them for answering. His mother said, "Patrick had stomach issues the last year or two before his passing. Looking back, we now know that was a sign of anxiety. We had him thoroughly tested for every possible issue, but never received a solid diagnosis. This was clearly a warning sign."

In fact, his last full day he stayed home from school with a stomach ache. Then in speaking with some of his friends, they remembered that he had in fact said goodbye to some of them in a way that seemed ominous in retrospect.

Finally, they also learned after the fact that he was having some very specific and emotional conflict with teachers. His dad said, "As you know, he had issues with a teacher or two, and later we heard he expressed his issues with the teachers. He was upset that they were going to be tested on material that hadn't been taught, and he really felt this wasn't right."

Again, there was no overlap between school and home to put out that fire. No one realized, I guess, how bad that conflict was. If they'd known they could have tried to buffer it or somehow get involved.

I think it's important to note here that students and teachers are inherently going to have boundary conflicts, timeline conflicts, and grading conflicts. All those are normal. This just serves as an example of how linking the different perspectives with more regularity, as more of a standard operating procedure as a school community, could help save lives. Then certainly, the dialogue would occur more, and you'd get more information. You may even uncover something going on with a student and thereby prevent another tragedy.

Possible Warning Signs

Parents, teachers, and any adult can look for certain signs that could indicate a teenager should see a doctor or a clinician regarding their mental health. Possible signs could be:

- Withdrawal from the family system.
- Withdrawal from their friend group.
- Unexpectedly quitting former passions, like a sport they loved to play.
- Changes in sleep patterns; perhaps they're always tired or they never sleep.
- Changes in eating patterns.
- Grades suddenly plummeting.
- Changes in study habits or overall motivation.
- Engaging in reckless behavior like using drugs, or drinking.
- Getting into a weird, obsessive-like relationship with technology.
- Giving away their possessions.
- Having uncharacteristic aggression.

Basically, any abnormal indicators could be warning signs. When I'm working with families I often hear, "That's just typical teenage behavior." Yes, any behavior could be a one-off, but if items from the list appear with regularity, the underlying issues need to be analyzed with clinical care. I also believe that any of those signs in isolation, especially if it only happens once, could be only a brief, passing disturbance.

As a school system, and also as parents, we like to maintain structure with consequences. But if we're simply responding with consequences, rather than stopping and looking to see where a behavior is coming from, that can just escalate the problem. Of course, with Patrick we know that he wasn't withdrawn from his family, he wasn't giving up in school, and he wasn't aggressive. Sometimes warning signs can be harder to spot than we might expect.

Patrick is a great example of why we need to take our kids to the clinician as much as we take them to the dentist. Commonly, children and teenagers are more likely to express their worries, fears, or concerns to adults who are not perceived as consequence-issuing, or freedom-restricting individuals. Furthermore, the therapists can screen for warning signs while building coping skills in their adolescent clients.

Pushing vs. Encouraging

> Patrick clearly felt that there is incredible pressure in our community (and in many communities) to achieve high academic status, which will translate to entrance into an elite college or university. In Patrick's final letters, he decried this mentality. Not everyone is cut out for college, let alone the elite few schools that our students strive for. Parents and students must realize that every student's path is unique, and there is no one definition of academic success.
>
> —Patrick's mom

In my experience working with parents of middle and high school students for the last 16 years, they are coming from a place of love. Typically, parents want for their children what they didn't have. Maybe they didn't have parents who could talk to them about college, or pay for college, or who even wanted them to go to college in the first place. Or maybe they're trying to replicate the success in life that they feel they had. "Well I went to this college, and I have this great life now, so I need my child to have that too." That's the "college carrot" I referenced earlier.

As an example of this, I was working with a father and son, and the father really wanted his son to go to USC. He was pushing for him to go there, yet the son had no interest. The son looked at the data points of

USC admissions, and he looked at his reality. As a student athlete and a balanced person, he had good grades and was doing well, but not to the point where he would solidify admission to a school like USC. I had to gently point out to the father that in 1991, when he got into USC, the admissions rate was approximately 70%. Now, it's in the low teens.

Times have changed, and again, parents want to know that their kids are going to be okay. As a school system, we need to remind them that there are over 4,000 colleges in the US. There are other schools that are great schools besides the one that we think about. Just like brands of food. We have our go-to brands because they're historic and public facing, but that doesn't make them the best brands. It just makes them the ones that we know.

When I make an effort to educate parents as opposed to judging their knowledge gaps, the conversation changes. They simply didn't know. They were operating on old information, but they're hungry for new information. Parents are doing the best they can and working with the tools they have in their toolbox. When the tools don't work, we have to give them new ones.

Parents can become trapped in the same cycle of behavior as the larger school community in that they want their child to live up to their full potential. Sometimes, that means that they expect their child to get a certain grade, take a certain level course, or be in a certain amount of activities. Of course, you want to encourage your child to challenge themselves and to be social and active. But there's a difference between this and pushing them to take classes, or be in sports or activities that they have no desire to be in. And helping parents achieve balance within their parenting approach is key.

Challenge Success

After Patrick's death, everybody took a big step back and began to reexamine the fundamental building blocks of the school culture and the greater community. What were their value systems? What level of pressure were students overall experiencing? What were social priorities?

The school community took steps to reevaluate and began to modify systems and norms within the school and the greater community. This was both to prevent another tragedy, and to deescalate the level of tension that had been simmering for years.

As one of these steps, the school district partnered with an organization called Challenge Success out of Northern California. Challenge Success is a great example of using a third party to help audit a school culture. What systems are working, and what systems aren't working? Those questions are traditionally reserved for academic features of the school campus. The goal of programs like Challenge Success is to pivot the conversation of internal change from academic specifics and data, to include the social-emotional aspects as well.

Challenge Success was founded to help reevaluate the way that school cultures operate and help schools reimagine how they define success. This circles back to how Patrick felt the markers for success were very much tied to certain data points. Challenge Success challenges stakeholders to look at how, why, and what type of success is rewarded.

In working with schools all over the country, I see many students battle academic stress, sleep deprivation, academic disengagement, cheating, etc. Essentially kids are going through the motions of being a student without any intrinsic attachment, care, or understanding of why they're doing what they're doing.

A very simple example of a change that a school might make to address some of this is the relationship with online grading platforms. Just like social media and the Internet, in many schools, grades are available online 24 hours a day. Yet the reality is that grades don't change in real time, necessarily. For example, you might have a missing assignment. And that missing assignment might register as missing for a week online even though you turned it in the next day. The teachers have 100 + students on their roster, so it takes time to grade, process, and input all those marks.

The issue with the 24-hour online system is that not only were kids feeling the pressure in the school setting to do well for the teachers and keep up with their friends, but then they would go home and also face that burden from their parents. "Why do you have a B? Why is this missing? What does this mean?" There was no time for decompression.

One of the changes I recommend is limiting access to online grades. Doing this creates a buffer. It decreases the freneticism of both the students and their parents feeling anxious about grades on a daily, even hourly, basis.

I also recommend implementing more parent education programs. What parents want to know is what they don't know. Because parents don't know what they don't know, it can be difficult to ask the right questions or take directives to do things differently. In other words, when the school has an expectation that parents modify how they're parenting their child, then parents would like to be armed with information, tools, and strategies about how to do that.

Parent education could be about signs to look for depression, anxiety, or suicidal ideation. Or, how do you talk to your child about college? How to talk to your child about disappointment? How do you make sure not to confuse your academic goals for your child's?

Essentially, though, Challenge Success is just one example of a third-party organization that can help you reexamine your school culture. Certainly, Challenge Success requires a financial investment and that might not be feasible for every school site or school district.

There are other options, such as partnering with neighboring districts and setting up a committee that can go in and audit another school district, and vice versa, creating more of a collaborative model. You don't have to wait to hire a third party to come in and help you start to sort out where you can do better and make changes.

Finally, keep in mind that bringing in a third person entity like Challenge Success is really only a first step. The school then has to actually implement these changes.

Patrick's Purpose

I can only imagine the pain and the grief that settles in a family after losing a child. For Patrick's family, the focus is now on learning how to heal and stay connected. With Patrick's Purpose, they've found a way to position their energy and pain to shine a light on others' mental health needs. They hope to prevent others from going through this experience.

Patrick's Purpose was founded by the Turner family after Patrick's death. It's a non-profit organization that strives to destigmatize teenage mental health. It promotes kindness and human compassion, and it celebrates soft skills instead of product-markers. They strive to pivot the conversation to help us better understand the attributes that we can and should celebrate in our youth while simultaneously calling us to action. We need to take mental health in teenagers seriously and that requires the community organism to reimagine our relationship with mental health. In his mother's words,

> Patrick's Purpose Foundation aims to promote mental wellness in schools and create a student-driven culture of kindness through educational programs and initiatives. Additionally, we award scholarships to students who attend a vocational school or community college, which would be considered an alternative path in our community. Patrick wanted everyone's journey to be uniquely their own, and we hope to honor his wish in our scholarship program.

This is one of the features of their organization that I really love. It sends the message: "Although you have chosen this path that is not the norm, or perhaps not highly regarded, it is equally important and meaningful. And we're proud of you." Patrick's Purpose is now expanding its reach to offer outreach and scholarship opportunities beyond their neighborhood and local school district.

I'm so inspired by the work that they're doing in our community. It's fantastic and meaningful and needed. This is why I'm partnering with Patrick's Purpose, as I stated in the Introduction, by donating 10% of all proceeds from this book to further their objectives.

Patrick's Purpose has received support from the overall community, and within pockets of the school. For example, his football team, a high school counselor, and various other staff members have lent their time and efforts to forwarding their message. However, the Turners would have liked more support from the school and the district itself. According to Patrick's dad, "It felt like we had a communicable disease. Some folks were great but it was like they didn't want the administration to know they were talking to us. Honestly, it felt like instead of leaning into a deeply painful and uncomfortable topic, they elected to retreat altogether."

On a march to bring awareness to teenage mental health, held on Patrick's birthday nearly two years after his death, hundreds of local community members and students from the high school came. But there was little to no representation from the larger school community. Generally, those attending walks, runs, marches, and the like, do so when they feel a sense of personal connection, investment, or ownership of a cause. As an attendee and supporter of Patrick's Purpose, I was thrilled with the remarkable turnout from the community, and admittedly disappointed with respect to the school perspective.

Conclusion

Ignorance is not a solution. There are too many resources, too much information, and too many methods to combat teenage mental health issues, specifically in schools and within our homes. It's about connecting to catch, with all adults in a young person's life coming together to keep an eye on them.

In the next chapter we're going to focus on communication between school and home. How can educators open the channels for parents? What are some strategies educators can use to reach out, and strategies parents can use to most effectively communicate when in crisis? We'll also look at some signs educators can look for that indicate it's time to reach out to parents, if they haven't already done so. In the meantime, please visit www.recoveredu.com for the book study, supplement resources, and relevant links that accompany the content of this chapter.

CHAPTER FOUR

Communication and Partnership Strategies

With Kaley in the first chapter, we were able to identify a mental health issue and mobilize. We were able to collaborate within the school and get her through her struggle with an open, communicative process. With Patrick's family in the last chapter, they didn't have a lot of information, and to no fault of their own. Patrick seemed fine at home, and they lacked a clear understanding of the struggles he was experiencing at school.

Kaley and Patrick's stories both demonstrate the importance of communication in very different ways. In the first, communication is achieved, and we have an opportunity to solve and support. But without that open channel of communication, we can suffer a tragic loss.

The Importance of Establishing Channels of Communication

With mental health and addiction, we're all victims of the secrets we keep. Often, parents don't want to share information that's deeply personal, for obvious reasons. Yet this means they're withholding information that's crucial for the school to properly care for, support, and facilitate that child's education. Whereas, for the parents that do want to communicate—and there are parents that are very willing—it's crucial to establish clear channels of communication with pathways parents can easily navigate.

It's very typical that parents under stress are not thinking clearly about communicating with the school. They don't know where to start, or who to contact. They don't know how much to say, and they're not sure of the reception they're going to get. It's very common for me to work with families who assume that their child will be judged, treated unfairly, ostracized, or in some way punished for the struggles that they're going through.

But what I've discovered working in education is that when schools are provided with real time information from families in crisis, they're more likely to respond than not.

From an educator's perspective, the challenge that we face is that families often wait until a problem has become so heavy and complicated before they involve the school. At that point, they drop a data bomb. Or maybe it's a situational scenario that's very hard to manage because of all the layers that need to be unpacked and evaluated.

More often than not, these crises build gradually. So, it might start with a student suffering from ADHD, and then they suffer a concussion. And then through the concussion it's discovered that they're suffering from anxiety and depression, and then we discover that they're self-medicating by using marijuana or other substances.

As an example of how detrimental a lack of communication can be, I worked with a Sophomore in high school who experienced only one of those issues above. They were an athlete with good grades, and suffered a brain injury via concussion during practice. As a result, they had a very hard time keeping up in class. They had issues with regular attendance, work completion, and communication. For about six weeks this student's ability to function dissipated significantly.

However, there was no communication from the family to the school. The school was making assumptions about the student: they must be doing drugs. Something must be going on. But even so, the school was not communicating these concerns with the parents.

And the parents were trying to figure it out on their own. This was their oldest child, and their first in high school. They had no idea what to do or where to begin. They didn't really grasp how severe the issue was and the problems it was causing academically. They also didn't understand the importance of communicating with the school, other than to call in an absence.

Again, these are things that from 30,000 feet we think ah, that's so obvious that you would communicate with the school. But parents who are really concerned and very invested are often in a problem-solving kind of survival mode. Common sense steps can elude them, and it's not their fault. Especially if there are barriers to communication, as there were in this situation. Unfortunately, it took everyone a long time to begin collaborating, and the situation got worse before it got better.

Obstacles to Parent Communication

When I am working with parents and trying to help them communicate effectively, preemptively, and consistently with the school site, the primary obstacles include the following:

- They don't know who to share the information with.
- They're fearful of not being taken seriously, of teachers being unresponsive, and what will happen with information shared.
- They don't want to share too much too soon, or they try to keep things on a need-to-know basis, so they only share what they think the school needs to know.

The problem with that last one is that at the end of the day, parents don't know what the school needs to know. But the deeper issue is that essentially, everyone is operating in isolation. The parents are trying to problem solve and manage in isolation, and the school site is continuing to manage how they've always done it. Neither party is communicating clearly until the need becomes so elevated that there is no choice but to communicate. For instance, if it's the end of the semester and the student is failing one or more classes.

Unfortunately, at that point it's too late for the school to say retroactively, "Oh, okay. We can go back and change those grades and let them make up those assignments and problem solve with you." That time has already passed. That ship has sailed. Subsequently, parents feel unsupported by the school, and the school feels ambushed by the parents. No one is happy, and we're left without a real solution.

How Educators Can Open the Pathways

There are two effective ways that schools can get parents involved. One is to establish very clear pathways of communication for parents. The other is to combat perceived fears.

The first is fairly simple. Pathways for communication can be included in the student handbook, on the website, on handouts at back to school night, and on individual teacher's websites. The messaging can essentially say, "Hey, if things aren't going well, or if you have a confidential issue that's affecting learning, this is exactly who you talk to and this is how you talk to them. When you talk to them, this is what you can expect from us in return: We will acknowledge your email, set up a meeting, and implement informal accommodations while we explore getting formal accommodations."

With these guidelines clearly in place, you already begin to assuage the worry of the parents because they have a very clear understanding of how to initiate communication in the event that they need to.

Parents should know:
- Exactly who to talk to.
- What the protocol is.
- What sort of information they should be disclosing.

- How should they disclose that information?
- That confidentiality will be enforced. (Ensure them of this!)

The second way to get parents involved would be to do some public relations initiatives to combat perceived fears that their child will be treated differently, negatively, or somehow become isolated. Another fear is that the information that they share will somehow leak to outside parties.

Especially in high performing affluent communities, parents and students are very concerned that what they share will then be shared with colleges. A huge fear is that if my son or my daughter has a mental health or an addiction issue in high school, their likelihood of college admission will decrease. When in reality, that type of information is guarded. It is protected and not something that travels with them to those other parties.

Strategies for Parents to Communicate

Release of Information (ROI)

One strategy that I encourage parents to utilize is obtaining a release of information. This is a great way to easily pass on information between the medical provider, family, and the school site. This requires the family signing a release of information form so that the psychologist, psychiatrist, medical doctor, or medical facility can have direct communication with the decision maker. Typically, the decision maker is the assistant principal, but it could even be a principal, or perhaps a guidance counselor. This allows them to quickly pass on any validating documentation necessary for teachers.

I'm not talking about medical reports here. They're not sending full medical charts or anything like that. What they send are letters verifying the need for extended time or a reduced school day. They might explain how such an accommodation would support that student in the learning environment.

This also removes from the parents the pressure of feeling like they have to understand how to translate the diagnosis and the clinician's findings—and to pass all that on appropriately, effectively, and in a timely manner to the school site.

Again, we're talking about elevated levels of care. We're not talking about a student who has a one-off anxious day. We're talking about students who are chronically and clinically affected with mental health or addiction issues.

Have Documentation Ready

When parents say, "My child needs extra time," the school replies, "And I need a letter from a doctor." That's a very simplified version of an exchange that can create a lot of tension and a lot of confusion. And it can occupy a lot of time, which could otherwise be used toward progress.

So, something to keep in mind as a parent is that when you make a claim, state a need, or debrief the school site, it's really important to already have ready the supporting documentation that will later be required. Again, that could be the letter from the physician, a documentation of doctor visits, or recommendations from the doctors that your child does in fact need a reduced day, extended time, or a higher level of care outside of the school environment.

Commonly, parents will express those needs to a school site void of any supporting documentation or medical validation. When ultimately the school will need documentation to be able to leverage policies and access loopholes within their procedures to give grace and make exceptions for a student.

Schools can communicate what documents they need through a simple checklist posted on their counseling website or in their student handbook. "If your student is experiencing x, y, or z, these are the types of documentations that are very helpful for us to be able to quickly mobilize and best support your child." The parent can then even just email a PDF of a letter from the clinician directly to the guidance counselor.

This is far more effective than the parent going to the guidance counselor stating the needs, and the guidance counselor saying, "Well this is what I need from you." And then they go back and forth from there. In this scenario, the parent then has to go back to the clinician and get a letter. The same goes for the back and forth of an email chain or duplicating meetings that could be done in one sitting. Meanwhile, the symptoms and the reality of that student's need may have worsened.

Clarifying the needs from both parties in a documented, formatted, and systemic way will increase the speed at which we can all support and help our students.

When in Doubt, Contact the Guidance Counselor

I highly recommend that parents have regular communication with their student's guidance counselor. The guidance counselor can disseminate information quickly. They can do so with authority, and with perceived validity from the staff and the teachers. In this way, the counselor can help drive the process.

The guidance counselor knows what the resources are, and they can help the parents determine when to get teachers involved. The counselor can help organize more of a uniform process rather than a game of pinball where parents are going from teacher to teacher at the last minute in a panic. This generally happens when parents are overwhelmed, and don't know where to begin. The counselor can help with all of this.

A parent does not need to send individualized email to all the teachers, or even a bcc to all of them. They can communicate directly with the counselor. And it is crucial that any information regarding issues impacting that student's learning or their ability to function like a typical peer in the school setting is communicated to the counseling staff.

If a parent keeps the guidance counselor in the loop and updated with any necessary documentation, then it's easy enough to contact the guidance counselor and say, "Hey, my child has been absent from school for two weeks. I need to have these absences excused and the opportunity to redo this work. My child also needs extra time and to take this exam they missed without penalty." If the school already has the proper supporting documentation, they can grant that quickly.

Strategies for Partnering with Parents in Crisis

The following strategies are the most effective ones I've found for partnering with parents in crisis. I've discovered them through my work over the last several years serving as a liaison for families in crisis, through my experience as a high school administrator, and through running an alternative high school for kids who have come out of crisis.

Have a Clear Point Person on Both Ends

Each school site should have a clear point person within that school who is the liaison for families in crisis. In other words, when a family is in crisis they need a clear understanding of who to communicate with. If not, we again go back to the pinball scenario, where parents are trying to communicate with anyone who they can get a hold of. It can be very frenetic because they're emotional and feeling a need to get things done quickly. The emotional response from parents can create tension with teachers who interpret this behavior as disruptive, rude or demanding.

When information is sensitive, it's much more effective for one person in the family in crisis, or one person on behalf of them, to likewise communicate with the school. That could be a parent, a clinician, or someone like me in the capacity of a consultant. The designated communicator should set themselves up with the clearly identified point person at the school, and they will be the two who communicate.

The primary communicators on both ends keep all the information organized and all of the needs met. This is more efficient and effective than trying to spray communication amongst a lot of people with huge bcc emails or reply-all emails. These can elevate family worry, school worry, and overall confusion.

Parents are much more likely to communicate when they know the one person they can communicate with, what type of information that person requires, and what kind of support that person can deliver on the back end.

Don't Take Things Personally

When supporting families in crises, sometimes you have to work really hard not to take things personally. Parents who are in crises can be fighting for the life of their child. With that comes a huge wave of emotional burden, even agony, for lack of a better term. They will posture aggressively, they will posture emotionally, and they will posture defensively. It's not uncommon for them to lash out and even make personal attacks.

If there's ever a family for which to give grace and to not take things personally, it is with the family in crisis. The power of human communication, connection, and compassion is undeniable. I've said this before, when a student or a family has the validation through expressed words in an email, or a conversation is directly written to them, they're more likely to accept help and lower their shields, even become vulnerable. And in this case, that means reading between lines of emotional responses, and identifying their core needs to best support the child and student.

If You See Something, Say Something

As a practice, in this day and age of crime and terrorism, we see signs everywhere that say, "See something, say something." This goes back to training teachers on how to have an uncomfortable conversation or write an email that's both assertive yet kind. Being able to confidently and lovingly reach out to a parent or even check in with a student and say, "You know, I've noticed these factors about you, and it's raised a flag for me. I just want to make sure you're okay. I want to make sure you're checking in with somebody either here at school or outside."

We're often afraid to say something because it's uncomfortable, and we worry we'll offend someone. But you also might save their life. You could be the first adult to see that student and that they're struggling. We watch our students come in and out of the classroom all day long, but a lot of students don't feel seen. Checking in with them can provide validation and connection, and lead them to appropriate supports.

Be Proactive

Things ended all right with the student I mentioned towards the beginning of this chapter with the concussion. But they could have gone better sooner had the parents or teachers been more proactive in their communication.

Eventually, the parents came to see me, and I helped them get organized, mobilized, and to establish communication with the school. At this point, the school was then able to support them. The teachers largely were very supportive, except for one. This one teacher felt that the parents had waited too long to provide information and was unwilling to let the student retroactively use medical excuses for missed assignments and assessments.

The student ended up doing very well at the end of the semester in all classes except for that one in which the teacher would not budge from their procedures and policies because the medical documentation was retroactive and not in real time. Again, being proactive helps parents avoid this reaction from overworked teachers lacking the time, energy, or patience to grade long-past assignments and rework grades.

In this instance, both parties were guilty in their own way. Remember, the parents weren't doing a good job communicating with the school. Yet the stakeholders in the school hadn't acknowledged the change in behavior or productivity. It was a silent standoff. Nobody was saying anything, and at the student's expense.

The teachers had observed that the student was missing a ton of class. The parents weren't perfect about calling in, so sometimes absences were unexcused; sometimes they were excused. Overall, the attendance was spotty. But more than that, the work completion was far below normal. The student was at school more than they weren't there. But their work habits in at least a couple of their classes went from nearly 100% completion to almost 100% incompletion. They were also scoring much lower on assessments than they had previously. And this went on for six weeks.

Now, having been a teacher with 180 students on my roster at any given time, I appreciate how much teachers have on their plate. But there were signs indicating that something was amiss. It's possible the teachers lacked information. Perhaps they hadn't been trained on the effects of a concussion or how to pay attention to mental health. So they proceeded as they would with any other typical peer by holding the lines and issuing consequences. This is what happens when the school has no information from which to operate.

Signs for Teachers to Reach Out

I recently led a staff in-service at a charter school district on how to track student indicators from an academic perspective. In that training, what we came up with was a simple checklist of five questions. The five questions are things for teachers to think about if they're noticing a change in behavior. These five questions are:

- Is there a drop in attendance?
- Is there a drop in participation?
- Is there a drop in homework completion?
- Is there a drop in test scores?
- Is there a drop in communication?

Note that participation and communication are different. You might have a student who regularly participates in class but doesn't really communicate. What you're trying to notice is if these five variables have dropped consistently at roughly the same time. If three or more of these have dropped synchronously, then it's time to send an email with those observations to the parent cc'ing the guidance counselor.

What to Do if a Parent Won't Act

The big question is what happens when you've reached out to a parent and they're not helping? The student is demonstrating red flags, and either they're just not responding, or they refuse to recognize or take it seriously. What should you do if they fail to act?

First of all, if you have a crisis in real time, such as a student who's actively ideating suicide and threatening to take their life—you would conduct a threat assessment. Many school sites have a trained threat assessor, typically a guidance counselor or a school psychologist. You would walk the student to the office and then they would go through the process with that approved assessor in a confidential setting.

From a legal perspective, you are their parent during a school day. This is the obligation of the school site. So, beyond a crisis in real time, county resources often have a mobile team that can come to the school site and check in with the kid. The team can even go to the student's house and do a welfare check. And this is where we often get stuck as educators. We worry about parents' reactions. Often we're afraid that we're overreacting, so we do less than we should. But I would rather have us overreact than fail to react.

Schools typically have a student support team. And if they don't, they should. The student support team typically consists of the student's core content teachers, guidance counselor, the school psychologist, and an administrator. Even without the parents, they can meet as a team to compare notes, record observations, and formalize those into documentation which they could then submit to the parents or to a local family services department if they feel like neglect is at play.

It's better to be safe than sorry. If you have a student that you worry may harm themselves or somebody else, it's unconscionable, in my opinion, to return them to an environment in which they're going to be absent of any form of support—even if that's their home. When parents won't act, they most certainly do after you've elevated it to that level. But this isn't something you would typically do.

A more common occurrence is that there's a crisis at school and you just can't get a hold of the parent. They're traveling, or they're working, or they just don't have their phone and are unable to respond. Then you would go ahead and facilitate the threat assessment and make sure that the child is safe, with an adult, and out of harm's way.

With the elevated process I talked about previously, keep in mind that really this would only manifest after parents have been presented with information and given opportunities to come to a meeting, to provide documentation, or to receive services either locally at the school or within the city context.

You wouldn't just go from, "Oh, I sent them one email and now I'm calling the county." That would be a worst-case scenario after you've done everything else you can do. If you're really worried about the student and after receiving information the parents still aren't willing or able to perform the necessary tasks, keep appointments, or take steps to insure the safety and welfare of their child—then you need to be willing to sacrifice that relationship with the parent in order to preserve the life of the child.

Conclusion

The most important takeaway of this chapter is that communication is essential. Parents need to know when to communicate, why and what to communicate, as well as how to communicate it. Every stakeholder on a school campus should also know at what point they need to communicate, why it's important for them to communicate, and what that communication looks like. This is to protect themselves from a liability perspective, to protect the integrity of the school site, and also, and most importantly, to protect the health and welfare of students.

I think what's crucial to understand is that we tend to minimize the impact one adult can have on the life of a child. Josh Shipp is an amazing author and speaker with a platform on the philosophy that it only takes one adult to change the life of an adolescent. Anyone on a school campus has this amazing opportunity to be that adult. But we're so busy just getting through our day that we forget our significance. Humility is important, but so are you and so is your ability to change lives.

At the same time, I know that education is a minefield of adults who are also struggling with mental health and addiction. The isolation, stress, and the fiscal reality of being an educator can create a perfect storm resulting in anxiety, depression, and substance abuse. Not only was this my experience as an educator, but I've come across it again and again in other educators I've gotten to know over the years.

In the next chapter, I'm interviewing a teacher and principal named David Schmitou. He's an author and advocate of mental health. We'll be learning about his experience managing his own mental health as an educator. I will also be sharing my own story as a call to action for educators to deal with their own stuff. At work, you're charged to care for these kids, but who's taking care of you? In the meantime, please visit www.recoveredu.com for the book study, supplement resources, and relevant links that accompany the content of this chapter.

SECTION THREE

The Educator's Voice

What educators want parents and other educators to know.

- The importance of us, as educators, facing our mental health and addiction issues.
- The role parents play in official student accommodations.
- Why communication continues to be key, as well as keeping an open mind.

CHAPTER FIVE

What Educator's Wish We Knew

There's a phrase that I love right now, which is "check on your strong friend." Not everyone with a mental health disorder, or an addiction disorder, will advertise it. In fact, frequently, the people who are at the highest levels of success are struggling at the greatest deficiencies. That said, it's imperative to understand how to leverage a conversation. Not a one-to-one conversation, but as a school community, and as a greater community.

How do we make the conversation of mental health and substance addiction more commonplace? How do we make it more accessible, and then through that, how do we achieve more meaningful change in the culture, the health, and the vibrancy of those who are supporting our kids?

With addiction, it's an "it takes one to know one" type scenario, I've discovered. So, while living with my addiction and knowing full well that I was addicted, it was easy to identify people in my life that I thought were walking a parallel path as me. Even then, I didn't have the confidence to say something to them, like, "Hey, let's get support together. Let's work on this together," in the way that a staff might view a weight loss challenge or a fitness challenge—in this congenial and collaboratively supportive way.

The topics of mental health and addiction are so taboo, so shielded with shame that there's very little peer-to-peer adult support in the education culture. But there's no reason people can't feel supported, loved, and welcomed while trying to make strides to improve their life. This will elevate their educational practice, which will increase their ability to properly educate and care for students.

Coach

The hard lesson I've learned about adult mental health in the educational setting, especially, is that sometimes there are no signs or symptoms, and it can still end in a worst-case scenario. My former colleague that I'll call "Coach" is one example. I served as the assistant tennis coach, and he was the head tennis coach. I became the assistant principal, and his boss, but we were still very good friends. We'd worked together for 11 years, and we still talked all the time.

When I first arrived, Coach was the authority figure, the mentor to me. Then I got sober and really focused on my mental health, got a promotion, and our roles shifted, even flipped. He was asking me questions, and I was providing some guidance and mentorship to him, despite the age difference. Nonetheless, he was one of my best friends.

When he took his life, I had no idea it was coming. It was very public, and very dramatic, and I was completely blindsided by it. I was emotionally devastated, obviously. It knocked me off my feet, and I knew I needed to use it as momentum to make a difference because I couldn't explain it any other way. That loss was the first of the dominoes to fall, and ultimately led to me resigning from my position at the high school that I had been at for 12 years.

The decision to leave was agonizingly hard, but I felt my experience losing such a close friend and a district employee, essentially at work, was largely disregarded by the chief decision makers. There was a glaring disconnect between their verbal statements of support and affirmation, and their nonverbal cues that my problems were better dealt with on my own, in silence, or elsewhere. And when I finally let them know I was going to take a leave of absence, my decision was greeted with verbal affirmations and nonverbal relief. I am not angry, but it does present a perfect example of antiquated thinking that associates mental health disorders with character flaws or moral defects.

I initially took a mental health leave with the intention of returning, but I never did. That seismic shift created an uncontrollable force within me, propelling me to extend my reach. I wanted to find a larger purpose within the educational space, so I started working with teenagers and families in a mentorship/coaching role. This allowed me to really focus on connecting kids to mental health and substance use resources, as well as teaching them to live a more authentic life.

As I've mentioned more than once in the book so far, I've had issues with mental health going back to my youth. I then turned to substances as I got older. In the next section, I will share this part of my story.

My Story with Mental Health and Substances

First of all, I think it's really important to understand that I was not a hot mess when I was working as an educator and using alcohol. I showed up to work. I was not using while I was at work. I did my job. I did it well. I was fully engaged. Again, I fired a lot of signs to those around me that I was doing well, similar to high school where I was struggling, but I would put up smoke screens that I was doing fine.

I remember early on going to school and being an athlete in elementary school. It was easier to manage depression and anxiety in those early years because kids are generally friendlier, and everyone's equally awkward. The pace and the levity of an elementary school setting is much easier to survive and traverse. Once I hit middle school, the social problems began.

But there was a paradox to my existence through middle school and high school in that on one hand, I was the recipient of relentless bullying from a very specific group of people at my school who just pounded me, and pounded me, and pounded me emotionally. There was very little physical violence, but mental warfare without pause—and really, without cause—for six years. Despite that, I was still earning nearly straight A's. I was starting on the varsity football team and the varsity tennis team. I had leadership roles in the student council, was very active with community service, always had a job, and maintained a brave and friendly exterior.

I had the markers, again, of what I called a 4.0 mask. This is a child who can present really well. Yet in reflection, it seems to me that a lot of the adults in my life must have been seeing the peer interactions, the lack of friendships, the isolation, and the loneliness and sadness. Yet very few wanted to investigate or see what was happening.

Therapy was never mentioned. It was not a topic of conversation. So, that resulted in me living in pure survival mode, white knuckled every day, all day, just try to get through school so then I could escape. Home, at least, was the safety zone. Of course, I was living in a time when there was no social media. People didn't have cell phones. The internet was just some weird thing that somebody had recently invented. I was able to effectively insulate myself within the family home, recharge, and reset.

That nightly reprieve is the only reason that I was able to survive. I'm confident that had I been a teenager with the technologies and the real-time information systems we have now, I would not have made it.

When I got to college, I decided to adopt what I would call "a chameleon effect," which was a complete overcorrection. I wasn't going to repeat high school, where I had few friends and was not socially accepted. Instead, I was going to be who I thought people wanted me to be. I dressed a certain way, joined a fraternity, and I would drink a lot and be very social.

I decided that being a 4.0 student hadn't worked for me in high school, so I was over that. My grades suffered tremendously, and that got me immediate results. I had friends, I was always busy, and I felt liked. But there was a vast divide between the optics I was presenting and my authentic self. It was no better than the opposite reality, in many senses, because I had to sacrifice who I was to position myself that way.

When I work with teenagers now, I see that teenagers and college students will often just ratchet their unsafe behaviors to a higher and higher threshold until it gets somebody's attention. For me, that was drinking to the point of blacking out and making very bad decisions. I would get hyper-emotional while intoxicated and create disruptions, either through losing my temper or melting down.

Then the next day, I would go into complete shame and regret mode, where I would simply pretend it didn't happen. I would avoid talking about it. I would avoid the people I had been around. I would go dark, essentially.

The chameleon phase lasted until my junior year of college, when I shifted to a parallel friend group. These friendships were different in that they could see me, and so they were able to have courageous conversations with me. I'm not saying that other people couldn't see me, but maybe they just didn't know how to say it, or they were only interested in that social friend. They weren't interested in having uncomfortable conversations. It was some of those people who really encouraged me to go see a doctor about my mental health.

I didn't know if I was offended or relieved. What I do know is that I went, and that was my first introduction to talking to somebody about how I was feeling. I learned there were options. So, through that junior and senior year of college, I was able to stabilize from the mental health perspective and have meaningful friendships.

I slowed down overall. I did well in college. I got A's and B's throughout. But even with that stabilization, drinking was still an issue. That was something that ultimately, I couldn't stabilize. I had to quit. When I finally made the decision to get sober, I was in my 30s.

When I finished college, I entered the workforce as a teacher. And the beauty of teaching for me was that I loved working with kids. Especially when I was teaching seventh grade, there's just this fiber of optimism and resilience in those kids. Many of them haven't been wronged often enough to become jaded, and that positive energy would fill me. At school, I felt very happy. But I was also very isolated, working in a classroom with only students. I had very little adult or peer interaction outside the passing period, or when I occasionally had lunch with other teachers.

I could keep my depression and my anxiety a secret. I could keep my drinking a secret. It wasn't until I moved over into the high school setting and I became a high school administrator that I began to have difficulty. I was trying to have conversations with kids, encouraging them to make better decisions, and I felt like a fraud. They'd gotten drunk at a football game, or they were using marijuana at school—and I would have to issue consequences and work with the family to find a solution. And in those conversations, I felt like a hypocrite because I knew that I was telling them to do something that I myself was not willing or able to do.

Now, again, from the mental health perspective, I was putting in the work. I worked with my therapist named Jessica, who saved my life, changed my life, and encouraged me to keep doing the work little by little. So, through therapy, medication, and setting some boundaries, I was able to incrementally get better, and better, and better. I reached a point where I felt confident enough to really face into the negativity alcohol was causing in my life.

I worked hard. I got sober. I found support. I felt great, but in the first six months that I was sober, I told no one I worked with. The only person who knew was my wife, because I felt so much shame that I had to be sober rather than pride that I was taking this transformative step.

The fear of judgment was weighing on me, and I didn't want to say anything until I felt confident that I could maintain my sobriety. So when I finally did tell people, they would say things like, "Yes. That connects a lot of dots." "I could tell something was up." "Yes, I had a suspicion. I could see it." These were people I was close to, many of whom I'd worked with for over a decade, but not one said anything to me at any point before that.

Dave's Story

Dave's story, from the mental health perspective, isn't too different from mine. I first came across Dave on Instagram. There are a lot of educators that I've come across on social media doing amazing work, largely and effectively self-promotional. There's a lot of idea sharing, and when I scroll through the feeds and read the blog posts, I often come away with, "Wow, that's really amazing. That's really polished and professional." The posts suggest perfection, and that they have it all figured out. Everyone seems to be living their best life, with no issues at play.

When I started connecting with Dave, I was impressed with the great ideas that he is putting into the world, beneficial for students and education in general. In addition to that, he offers up a layer of vulnerability, truth, and self-reflection that can be rare in the social media space. I felt called to include Dave's story in this book because he sets a great example of how we can blend success and vulnerability, without one outweighing the other. The following is in Dave's words.

My current full time role is The Executive Director of Curriculum and Instruction in a small school district located between Flint and Detroit, MI. I serve and support four building principals, 150 teachers, and 220 students. I am in my 20th year of K-12 education, having served in the past as a middle school teacher, assistant principal, athletic director, principal, turnaround principal, and an adjunct professor. I have my BS from Central Michigan University and my MA and EdD from Eastern Michigan University.

I grew up in a military family, requiring me to move around A LOT. As a result, I never had any enduring friendships. I learned how to make acquaintances really quickly, but I was always moving or my friends were always moving. As I went to middle school I received the label of "gifted," and as a result believed everything was supposed to come easily to me.

My first couple of years in the classroom, I was extremely arrogant. I thought I had all the answers and that I was the best teacher around. As a result, my peers and co-workers distanced themselves from me. I progressed through my career, oblivious to how I was acting.

Eventually it all caught up to me. As an adult, sometimes life gets hard, but I did not have the skills to manage the difficulties. I did not have friends to lean on and had no idea what it was like to truly struggle. I quickly started to spiral as a result. I tried to keep everything inside, but everyone knew I was struggling.

As a principal, I never wanted to be vulnerable. I never wanted my staff to see me shaken, so the more I struggled, the more I fought with myself. I eventually hit my breaking point when I realized the dark thoughts I was having were consuming all of my time and energy. Thankfully, I found myself in counseling, on medication, and eventually willing to embrace who I was, the struggles I faced, and am now using my story to try and help others.

Teachers are often afraid to be vulnerable, too. We have turned the profession into one where displaying a struggle, an insecurity, and weaknesses, is seen as a "gotcha". Teachers feel like they have to have all of the right answers all the time and despite our best attempts to force collaboration and networking, because of the system we have created, being real, open, and honest have become foreign concepts to so many.

> The reality is, we must practice what we preach. We want kids to focus on growth. We want students to embrace what could be not what was. The best way for us to demonstrate this to kids is to model it with our lives. The best teachers are those who reach out to others. Find someone you can confide in. Find someone you can lean on and NEVER feel like you have to do it alone.

I agree with Dave very much here. Speaking from experience, working on my mental health and my sobriety is a daily commitment, and it ebbs and flows. But I really think it's imperative. It's crucial. If you could take away just one thing from this entire book, I'd like it to be this: Look in the mirror and self-identify where you could do better, where you're not feeling 100%, and seek resources. We live in a world with so many resources that can help peel back the layers, from self-help books to virtual, anonymous resources, to one-to-one traditional therapy. It's never too late to make a change for the better.

Signs and Symptoms a Colleague May Need Help

Also, I would encourage the decision makers on a school campus or in a school district to turn the spotlight on everyone during conversations about mental health, as well as addiction. We need to move the spotlight from the student population so that it pans around and includes the adults. It's important to also teach them what the warning signs are, what their resources are, how to get help, and what help looks like.

Now, it's important to note that I am not a clinician. I am not a doctor. I'm not a mental health provider. But the signs and symptoms that I was manifesting and that I can recognize in a colleague are as follows:

- Arriving late to work.
- Arriving to work unprepared.
- Exhibiting unnecessarily isolative behavior.

- Avoiding adult peer-to-peer interaction during passing periods or breaks; lunchtime; before school or after school.
- Excessive irritability with students, to the point where the level of dissatisfied students and escalated conflicts in the classroom are at an abnormal level.
- Refusal to collaborate.
- Refusal to innovate or absorb new curricular benchmarks.

Of course, there are also the obvious signs like excessive weight gain or weight loss, bloodshot eyes, and so on.

Teacher Education

A primary goal here is to make the conversation regarding mental health and substances more commonplace for all stakeholders. Instead of itemizing an action point as specific to student culture or student life, include teachers and staff as well. Otherwise, you are ignoring the elephant in the room—the teachers, staff, and other professionals charged with caring for the students.

The educational platforms are going to look very different, of course, because the way you approach the subject with professionals is going to be different than the way you've approached it with kids. Nonetheless, it's important to have a tangible, reliable, and regularly scheduled education system with trainings and in services. These work to ratchet up the exposure on both sides of the fence to create a common language of signs, symptoms and solutions for both students and educators.

On this topic, I asked Dave what trends he saw in terms of professionals being more open and accepting of mental health/recovery in schools. Here is his response:

> With more and more conversations about Socio-Emotional Learning in schools, I have found more educators embracing "hashtag mental illness." I am afraid that the conversation has

become the new buzzword and as a result people are latching on to it, not necessarily for pure motives, but instead to appear relevant and trendy. Although this may help destigmatize the struggle, I am hopeful that it also doesn't water down what genuine support may really be needed for those fighting the battle.

Dave makes a great point regarding the optics of anything that's becoming trendy. In this case, it's mental health. I've said before, and I'll say it again: We talk a lot about talking about mental health. We need to be able to translate those hashtag sentiments into the school setting, but it's very difficult for a teacher to do that in isolation. It requires a systematic approach, whereupon the entire staff is educated and making a common effort to bring awareness to these issues. And not just on National Mental Health Awareness Day, or National Suicide Prevention Day—mental health is 365 days a year. It's not isolated to one day with a hashtag or a post.

I also asked Dave how he thought teachers could go beyond just speaking about empathy to applying it in their classrooms when supporting students with mental health and addiction conditions. He said:

> I am a firm believer that knowing the difference between EACH student and EVERY student is the answer. Realizing that every student has baggage. Every student has trauma. Every student has fears. Every student is a collection of each student. When we get to know each student as a person, not just a number, a test score, and a part of a collective class, then students will begin to feel valued, noticed, and hopeful about their unique destiny and future.

Challenge Day

A peer-to-peer program that both Dave and I highly recommend for students is Challenge Day. In Dave's words, "Challenge Day is an amazing program that encourages empathy and compassion." I would love to see something like this as professional development for teachers as well.

I've experienced Challenge Day as a teacher and watched my students go through the day-long process. For Challenge Day, the organization brings in expert facilitators who lead peers through shared exercises designed for them to start to see the reality of those with whom they don't normally relate. Students are often divided by grade-level, but break-out groups are purposefully blended to include different types of students—from different cliques, socio-economics, academic tracks and so on.

Students are then led through activities that allow them to understand that this person to my left and this person to my right, despite our differences, is struggling with similar things. It's about opening a dialogue and creating bridges. It's not going to be like a High School Musical, where now they all know the same dance, but what it does is it humanizes the connection, and it humanizes the struggles we are all facing but often at different levels.

Adult connections within a school would be similarly transformed if the staff could go through a similar type of programming at least once a year. The real magic of Challenge Day happens, I think, because it is done by an outside third party. It's not staff-driven or staff-led.

While I love staff-driven professional development, when you're really trying to affect change, bringing in someone from the outside who's trained and doesn't have a horse in the race, per se, does a much better job at facilitating that.

Conclusion

The main takeaway of this chapter is that mental health and addiction are not confined to socioeconomics, gender, age, or anything else. We really have to pivot our perception of mental health and addiction from being an us-versus-them situation, and absorb a mentality of "we." We all have mental health, and where we exist within its spectrum is unique and subject to change without notice. We all have a possibility of either being personally affected by mental health issues and addiction, of loving someone affected, or of working with someone. We have to command ownership and authority over our own struggles, and the resources available to confront those struggles, in order to create systematic change and a shift within the educational community.

It seems that mental health and addiction can be something of a chicken or egg type scenario. Which comes first? For example, I didn't engage in substance abuse in my childhood. But the mental health manifested, and the alcoholism came as a side effect of my lack of coping skills. I tried to self-medicate or self-cope or keep my feelings at bay. Or I would try very unsuccessfully to hide my emotions, or my feelings of anxiety and depression.

As an educator, when I started making a commitment to confront, to look inward, and to deal with these issues, I started with the mental health perspective. I worked with therapists whom I ended up seeing for well over a decade, every week. Only then did I eventually work up the courage and the resolve to face my reliance on alcohol.

Both of those decisions are certainly two of the most important decisions that I've ever made, and they made me a better educator. They made me a better high school administrator, a better husband, a better father, and a better friend. However, in hindsight I also understand that I was demonstrating lots of behaviors that should've been shouting to everyone to my left and to my right that things were not well. Yet virtually nobody reached out to me or segued into a conversation to check in on my mental health or my use of alcohol.

I think that was because it was super uncomfortable, and a conversation that the people who worked with me and who loved me didn't know how to have in a professional setting. As an educational community, we need to better understand the warning signs of adults that may be struggling. Educators need to know how to get help facing their mental health, and perhaps addiction, to become better professionals and live happier and healthier lives.

As Dave says:

I have heard many schools describe themselves as "a family," yet at the same time be unwilling to have critical and crucial conversations about work and about life. Families, today, understand there are no taboo conversations. It is the job of a family to rally around each other, to lift each other up, and to call each other out. If a teaching staff really wants to be a family, it is essential that each person owns his/her responsibility to be there for others, to lean in, to hold a hand, to have those hard conversations, and to offer support in good times...and in the bad.

In the next chapter we're going to look at specific procedures and policies that school sites, school districts, and educators can utilize, both formal and informal, to support the students in their school system who are struggling from mental health or addiction. Ideally these procedures should help educators become comfortable utilizing resources and pathways that decrease their likelihood of outsourcing our students to have somebody else care for them while they're struggling. I will urge educators to embrace a culture that supports those students while keeping them as present as possible, and as engaged as possible on their school site. We will address what educators wish parents knew as well. In the meantime, please visit www.recoveredu.com for the book study, supplement resources, and relevant links that accompany the content of this chapter.

CHAPTER SIX

What Educators Wish Parents Knew

In the last chapter, we talked more about educators and the importance of us acknowledging and tackling significant personal issues as a "we" rather than in isolation. This means asking for help and supporting colleagues in their efforts to be healthier and create a better learning environment for all students.

Now, we're going to focus back in on students, primarily supporting those with 504, IEP, or similar plans. In other words, those who need official accommodations. We will also discuss the role that parents play in official accommodations. What do educators want parents to understand about the process? And what strategies can educators provide parents to help build a cohesive team supporting that student?

A Case Study on Resistance

The process of obtaining accommodations can be arduous and time consuming. And with certain students under certain circumstances, the need for accommodations can meet with resistance. When a formal request for accommodations leads to conflict and students are not able to obtain those accommodations in a timely manner, it becomes a huge setback for their learning and for their future goals.

I worked with a family who had been attempting to receive accommodations for their child for over two years. The student had a lifelong struggle with visual processing in the dyslexia space, as well as auditory processing. In fact, in elementary school this student had been told at a parent conference by a teacher that the parents should expect that the student would never go to college. Talk about a blow to morale!

Throughout elementary and middle school this student had been sidelined. The family had to fight for additional resources to ensure their child was ready to integrate into a comprehensive high school setting. But when they arrived at high school, there was no acknowledgement of previous accommodations. It was as if the entire battle the student had waged to get there hadn't happened.

Regardless, the family kept fighting. For two years, they had been providing ample documentation, physician records, mental health records, and testing both through the school district and an independent testing company. Yet they were still caught in the bureaucracy of pinning down, identifying, and implementing accommodations for that student.

At this point, working on the outside of the school system was new for me. I had previously been an administrator and would have been sitting on the other side of the table. I would have been a gatekeeper, working with a team to determine if accommodations were necessary and if so, which ones. From this new position, it was alarming to witness the disconnect between the teachers at the table, the psychologist and the guidance counselor, and the family. Given the same information, they were all stuck with a different perspective of exactly how to support that student.

Meanwhile, the student was inappropriately placed in a science class. The class was well over the threshold both from a prerequisite perspective and a functional learning perspective. And the anxiety of feeling unsupported in this class, and in a comprehensive high school overall, led to very poor grades, low self-esteem, and a reluctance to attend school.

Adding to the student's anxiety, teachers were overall unwilling to give any sort of grace by way of unofficial accommodations while they were waiting for official accommodations. One of the decision makers on the team could not see the need for accommodations, and the teachers were afraid to cross them. Everyone was spinning in the bureaucratic turbine, and nothing was happening.

There was a high level of frustration and emotion from all sides, but particularly from the family. And what I came to realize is that while there was a breakdown in communication, no one was at fault. The key, I understood, was to teach them how to communicate with each other. I really worked with the parent and the student to communicate their needs and deliver the supporting documentation in a way that was not litigious or threatening. I urged the educators to communicate with the family in a way that was clear, concise, and human.

What do I mean by human? Well, many times we get caught up in edu-speak, or the lingo that educators know who are on those IEP or 504 teams. A parent doesn't know these terms, and a student certainly isn't familiar with them. They're confusing, even to other teachers, and they don't hold any more meaning than an alternative phrasing that a parent or student would be more likely to understand.

So I was able to coach the parties through how to communicate, by first establishing the basics of:

- Who do you communicate with?
- Where do you start?
- What kind of email do you write?
- How do you follow it up?
- What kinds of questions do you ask?
- How do you build that rapport and foster that relationship?

With communication protocols in place, we were able to resolve the situation entirely within six weeks. Accommodations were put in place, and the district was brought in to help mediate the school site team.

And now, two years later, this student is graduating from high school with very good grades and *will* attend college. They have a new lease on academic life with restored confidence. The accommodations were instrumental in this student's success. But even more than that, they were a gesture of teamwork and empathy, and an acknowledgement that not all students are the same.

This is why students that need accommodations should be given them, and not made to feel as if they are getting something for free or somehow getting a deal. Because at the end of the day, accommodations do not give a leg up, they simply level the playing field.

Accommodations - Liabilities and Mandates

Formal accommodations typically occur in a 504 plan or an IEP. These are legal documents, and the accommodations are not suggestions. They're mandates.

We've talked a lot about the importance of accommodations from an ethics perspective. From a liability perspective, educators are required to deliver these accommodations without making the student feel as if they're somehow burdening them. Because I guarantee you, that kid would do anything to not need an accommodation in this way.

If we make our students feel as if they're somehow being offensive, too needy, or otherwise bothersome, they're less likely to use those accommodations. They're more likely to feel shame about whatever condition they're dealing with, in addition to the demands of being a full-time student. This creates a level of toxicity, stress, and a feeling of isolation for the student within the classroom and even the larger school community.

That said, sometimes students can be resistant to using their accommodations, and through no fault of the teacher. When I work with families, I really work with students to embrace their accommodations. That doesn't mean they have to walk around the hallways telling everybody they have them. It's about reminding them that this is not giving you a leg up. This is just leveling the playing field and giving you a fair shot at comprehensive education.

Too often, the conversation with parents around accommodations is nonexistent. As an educator, you won't hear anything from anyone all semester. The student hasn't leveraged any of their accommodations, parents haven't said anything, and then towards the end of the semester when the grades are going to go onto that transcript, everyone comes out of the woodwork, trying to retroactively access them.

Both student and the parents have known about the accommodations the entire semester, yet, they're just now trying to utilize them in an effort to save the grade. So not only do educators need to set a tone in the classroom that the accommodations should be used—that they're helpful and valid—but parents also need to set this tone within the home. That begins with a simple acknowledgement of those supports to the student and asserting their implementation as the student progresses through curriculum.

Setting a tone within the home, especially, will build confidence in that student to practice self-advocacy skills. Students should use their accommodations early and often, and over time. This is much more effective than ignoring them and trying to pretend like they don't need them, and then at the 11th hour, trying to use them all at once. This really is not how accommodations are intended.

Additionally, if the student has accommodations but is not using them, and not doing well, a teacher can activate their implementation rather than waiting for the student to do so. I appreciate giving students autonomy, but when we aren't proactive, we end in reactive conflict more often than not.

Importance of Understanding Accommodations

My first two years of teaching, I taught in an urban inner-city school. Most of the student population came from low income households, where English was not the primary language. Accommodations were not part of the larger conversation, typically because of lack of parent involvement. Many parents worked multiple jobs, and there was both a language and an educational barrier.

But when I moved and I began teaching more affluent populations, the conversations of accommodations were commonplace. As a new teacher, I was given a list of accommodations and a list of students who needed those accommodations, and that was it. There was no translation. It was kind of like an IKEA model. "Here, you go and build it."

I didn't know where to start. I didn't quite know what they meant. And as a teacher, I really had no idea what to do with the accommodations or who to ask. It would have been helpful to have been connected to readily available support.

While schools will likely have a staff training maybe once a year where the special education department will talk about accommodations, it is often more of an info dump than a learning opportunity. I would find myself glazing over in these situations, and I couldn't absorb much of the information. It wasn't personal to me, and I didn't quite understand its value.

So, having a clear point person on every grade team level who is available does wonders. If an English teacher knows, for example, that they can reach out to the special education teacher on their grade level team, now they know whom to ask: "What does this accommodation look like? How would I best use it for this student? If this doesn't work, what are some other options?"

More of a coaching model like this would allow teachers to become fluent in the accommodations, rather than sticking them in a folder on the side of our desk that we only look at when a certain student asks for extra time on a test. It's important that we know more than just who has accommodations and what the specific accommodations are. We need to establish a protocol where we know:

- Who has them.
- What they are.

- Why they have them.
- Why they're beneficial.
- How to practice them.
- How to deliver them to your student to reach the maximum potential within that student's capability.

What Happens if You Don't Follow Official Accommodations

Essentially, if a teacher is not following accommodations, they could lose their job. The district certainly would be liable to a lawsuit. If the school is not meeting the criteria of a FAPE, which is Free Appropriate Placement in Education, then the student could then go to a private school on the offending school's dollar.

That's at a very dramatic level, of course. At a more commonplace level, the teacher would be held responsible for the lapses in the student's grade if they were denied the accommodations. And certainly, that student could be moved out of their class, their grade could be appealed, and they could be given the opportunity to redo any work completed without proper accommodations.

Not only is it unethical, but you'll get written up and otherwise held accountable from the overarching system of checks and balances within your school district. And it's embarrassing. You don't want to be labeled as that teacher who is ignorant to accommodations. I want to note here, I think it's particularly important to understand that there's a difference between a new teacher who doesn't know how to implement accommodations, and a teacher who is aware of those things, yet denies a student access.

For example, a common dilemma I hear about is when the student has an accommodation that lets them take a test in another setting. For a variety of reasons, the student is able to take exams in an alternate room from their peers, perhaps by themselves, proctored by another teacher or staff member.

But the teacher of record in their classroom will say, "Let's just see how you do on this test and if you don't do well, then we can retest later." And then two or three weeks will go by, and they'll get the results back from that exam. It's a B, an 84%. And then the teacher will say, "Well, you got a B on it, so actually you can't take it again with those accommodations." When the accommodations are intended to be used in the first place, not after the fact.

If they had taken the test with their accommodations, which they need and have been granted, they might have earned a different score that was more aligned with their best effort and their natural ability. Remember, the accommodations are set in place to level the playing field. There's no reason someone can't earn an A with accommodations.

What Educators Wish Parents Knew

Part of the dilemma in the case study I presented toward the beginning of this chapter was rooted in the fact that the parents had a historical negative association with trying to get support or accommodations for their child. This was based on that conversation with the elementary school teacher who told them the student would never go to college. Understandably, the parents entered the situation with defensive posturing and lacking knowledge of how to communicate effectively with the school system. This was through no fault of their own, since they weren't informed how to appropriately navigate the process.

Approach with an Open Mind

With that situation in mind, and in general, I think educators really want parents to approach the situation with an open mind, full transparency, and good faith. Just because they had a negative interaction with another teacher, doesn't mean they will have one with them.

The same thing can happen when multiple siblings from the same family progress through the same school. The older sibling might have had a great relationship with a teacher or a really bad experience with one. Or the family had negative interactions with teachers in general. So, when the next one comes up through the pipeline, again they're making assumptions and they're posturing aggressively, defensively, or passive aggressively. Or maybe they're not communicating at all because they feel like it's a waste of time and energy.

That can be really frustrating for educators because people do grow and change from one year to the next. In addition, just as any of us don't want to be guilty by association or defined by the person to our left or to our right, educators want to be given that same opportunity. This good faith is essential for educators to successfully problem solve with families. There has to be a level of civility in place, as well as transparency and a defined protocol for collaboration to be effective.

Don't Hold a Grudge Until You've Had a Conversation

As parents, do your best to trust the process, trust the teachers, and trust the system despite previous negative interactions. One rule of thumb vital for parents who may not think trust is possible: Don't hold a grudge until you have had a conversation.

In my previous book, *The Assertive Parent*, I wrote about this rule of thumb in depth. Parents will become frustrated, and maybe rightfully so. Regardless, they're frustrated with a decision or a teacher's policy. And rather than having a conversation with that professional, they elect to go all the way to the top. But when a parent goes over the teacher's head right away, firing off angry emails or making calls to the school district or to the principal, the person at the top ultimately is going to say, "Well have you talked with the teacher?"

If the answer is no, they send the parent back to the bottom to start over. Yet that teacher now knows that the parent went to their boss, and nobody wants to get told on to their boss unless they've had a chance to remedy it themselves. So now, the parent has alienated everyone along the way. They've also lost an opportunity to have that conversation which very typically does solve the problem.

And I will note here that it's important to sit down at a table for one of these conversations. This shouldn't be done over email or with a phone call, but face-to-face with the goal of gaining clearer understanding and opening lines of communication.

Advocating for Overextended Students

Although a lot of the content of this book so far has been aligned with areas of improvement, there are also many times where it's the educator who is advocating for the student. They're trying to carve out more empathy and space in that student's life, and it is the parent who is the driving force of the overextension, the stress, or the other factors hindering their education.

For example, parents who are very, very concerned with college admissions or grade point averages will essentially force their child to enroll in too many rigorous classes, or rigorous classes in areas that they're not passionate about. Without interest in the subject, they don't have any intrinsic motivation to learn. And when teachers see students in this situation, they often want to reach out. They think, "I wish I could tell that parent that they're putting too much pressure on their kid. I wish I could tell that parent that their student has no desire to be in my class."

Well, it's not about wishing. It's about learning how to say those things and to have those conversations without getting too combative. It's about being able to professionally advocate for that child, because those factors contribute to the mental health crisis we're experiencing. Again, parents don't know what they don't know, and if they are operating on an assumption or outdated information, it is a perfect opportunity to upgrade their paradigm.

When a teacher notices a situation like this, it's okay to ask questions. When possible, a teacher can work with the parent to assure that that student has the time, energy, ability, and the intrinsic motivation to really invest in the class. And I'm not talking about whether they can get an A. It doesn't matter if they get a C- in that class, so long as the student has a desire to be in it and has the time and space to be able to study the material and read the books.

Many of our kids are overextended, under motivated, and too heavily scheduled. The educator can often see this when parents don't.

Understanding Personal and Professional Boundaries

Teachers have the rare opportunity to be one of the most formative adults in a student's life. And teachers who can connect with students on a personal level are more likely to have them perform well academically by helping them develop motivation. Maybe the student wants to do well for that adult. Maybe the teacher even inspires them to like math, even though they never did before. And through that relationship, it's not uncommon for the student to start to confide in and share information with that teacher.

This is where the boundaries become very important. It's healthy, and it's totally fine to have that relationship where you are the listening ear for that student. But it's super important to remember to not overstep that boundary and become a therapist in lieu of one or become a resource in lieu of the specifically trained and licensed resource that that student needs.

It is also important to understand the rules of being a mandated reporter. If that student confides in you that they have been hurt by someone, or that they're planning to hurt themselves or somebody else, or that illegal activity is going on in the home and it's impacting their learning—teachers sometimes feel stuck.

This has happened to me as a teacher, being so fearful of breaking the trust with that student because of our great relationship. But I knew ethically, and really in the bigger picture, what was best for them was for that information to be delivered to the correct resources. They will be mad at you, but at the end of the day, it's better for them. It's better for their health, and it's going to keep them safe.

Rather than them feeling safe just in your classroom, the goal is to have them feel safe everywhere. And while that's not always possible, certainly, that's our working goal with every student.

Getting Help and Helping Others

Educators are amazing beings, in part because they make so many decisions every day. They're the ultimate multi-taskers, but this can also become overwhelming. So it's a very simple principle, but don't be afraid to ask questions.

When I was a teacher and I didn't know something, I could tell whoever was asking me, "Go ask the principal." And when I became the assistant principal and parents would come to me with questions, I had to get used to saying, "I don't know, but I'm going to find out and I'll get back to you." As an administrator, I really had to get used to not knowing all the answers.

So in the motion of your day, if you discover that you're not sure if you're correctly implementing accommodations, or how much autonomy you have to give an unofficial accommodation, or the best way to email a parent to express your concern that their child is suffering, overextended, over scheduled, or in a class for the wrong reasons—the answer's in the room.

You have a wealth of intellectual property on your campus. There are other teachers, stakeholders, counselors, and principals that have been doing this longer and more efficiently, perhaps. As such, learning to ask questions and seek help might make you feel vulnerable, because you are used to knowing all the information or having all the answers. But to create a more efficient system of teaching, learning to ask questions is always the best practice.

When you have many people in one ecosystem, as you do on a school campus—students, staff, parents, administrators—there's bound to be conflict and confusion. There are going to be times when people's individual philosophies or interpretations of rules or implementations of policies differ. That should be expected. But while we can expect that experience, we don't need to let that experience define us or create an expectation of conflict and confusion.

Conclusion

The topic of accommodations is just one subject within the larger topic of transparency and communication. It's important to have very clear channels of communication, establish protocol, and be willing to dialogue, compromise, and overall work towards a shared understanding. Rather than operating in an either/or philosophy, we need to adopt more of an "and" mindset.

I know when I was teaching, when students would reference seeing a therapist or perhaps even leave our school setting for more intense therapy or treatment for mental health or addiction, it was as if they went into the void. I didn't understand where they were going, what they were doing, or how that person, institution, or center would help them.

To help build this understanding for teachers, in the next chapter we're going to dig into the clinical professional's perspective. What is the perspective of the doctors and clinicians who treat our students suffering from mental health and addiction? And from the outside, how do they feel we, as educators, can do a better job supporting our students? What do they want us to know that we might not know already? In the meantime, please visit www.recoveredu.com for the book study, supplement resources, and relevant links that accompany the content of this chapter.

SECTION FOUR

The Clinician's Voice

What clinicians want educators, parents, and even students to know.

- What treatment can look like.
- What happens with different levels of care.
- Strategies for educators to best partner with families and clinicians.

CHAPTER SEVEN

What Clinicians Wish We Knew

Over the course of my time as an educator in middle and high school, I remember students leaving. They would go away, and maybe I would receive an email from a parent or from their counselor saying that they had temporarily, or even permanently, left school to seek treatment. It was like they went into this abyss, and I had no idea where they were going, why they were going, what they were doing, or what it looked like. I just knew that they were no longer at school.

So, in this chapter, we will examine what treatment looks like, who it serves, and what its objectives are. The intent is to provide you, as an educator or parent, a better understanding of the realities behind adolescent treatment. In the next chapter, we will then review all the levels of care leading up to residential treatment, which is the highest level.

The long-term goal of adolescent treatment is to rehabilitate and stabilize students so that they can go on to lead healthy and fairly typical lives. Returning to a school or a comprehensive education setting is generally the longer-term goal. Building context for educators is vital because not only are students leaving school to receive treatment, you may have students that will enroll in your class mid-year having returned from a therapeutic setting.

One glaring reality in education presently is that far more students are grappling with mental health disorders and addictive situations. Yet some educators and other adults have a propensity to disregard the data and assume that things like mental health disorders, anxiety, or even ADHD are trendy or being over diagnosed. They don't buy into those issues being significant or even substantiated. That kind of dismissive positioning of somebody else's struggle is an easy way to gaslight that relationship.

You can either pretend that the data markers don't exist and a mental health crises is not happening, or you can pivot, lean in, and try to understand more about how it's happening, why it's happening, and where it's happening.

Context lends itself to empathy, and empathy lends itself to connectivity. And connectivity, as we know, drives education. Context and understanding are touchstones for anyone interacting with a teenager or young adult who has received treatment. With understanding will come the empathy that will help you better support them in either their exit from or return to your school.

As I stated earlier, a lot of students would simply leave school. This was especially common with more traditional, or outdated, zero tolerance discipline models. When a student would have a run-in with drugs or alcohol in the school community, immediate expulsion was a common response. In other words, if you have a zero tolerance policy on your campus and a student has one run-in, you expel them. Then they move to a different setting.

When a student does indeed leave a school setting to receive a higher level of care or treatment, it should occur after every opportunity has been exhausted in that school setting to support, redirect, and adequately triage any difficulty that a student is going through. This is something I feel very strongly about.

If you haven't first tried to identify why they are using, or perhaps how their mental state is affecting or actually leading to use, you're doing a disservice to those children. You're creating a cycle of shame and a cycle of isolation, neither of which will solve the mental health or substance crisis that we're facing in schools.

Visions Adolescent Treatment Center

As I've stated earlier, since I left my career in comprehensive education, I've been working in the coaching and consulting world. Part of my job as a coach and consultant for families is to help them connect with needed resources. And several of those instances led to me assisting teenagers with seeking treatment for mental health or dual diagnosis substance abuse. And one of the places that I became really impressed with—based on the culture, the community, and the results of my clients who were going to treatment—was a company called Visions Adolescent Treatment Center in Malibu, in the greater Los Angeles area.

I would go and work with students at Visions while they were receiving treatment. Primarily, I would help them with their educational goals and manage communication between their home school and the treatment center. Through that I got to know Dr. Amanda Shumow, who is the co-owner of Visions with her husband Chris, and has successfully created a very unique company that she has run for the last 17 years.

And now, over the last year or so, I have become their education and curriculum specialist for the greater community. I coordinate the educational objectives and individual educational plans for students from all over the country and world who come to Visions, either for residential treatment or to attend their therapeutic day school in West Los Angeles.

One of the reasons that I wanted to interview Amanda and get her perspective on teenage mental health and substance use is because she is a progressive thinker and a thought leader in terms of the innovative ways that clinicians and treatment centers can work to rehabilitate. Visions focuses not just on the student, but also on the larger family system and all of the stakeholders in that child's life who are contributing positively and negatively, intentionally or unintentionally, to that child's welfare.

Amanda has lived an experience similar to those she is working with. As a student, she was kicked out of school, dismissed just that quickly when her behavior didn't match her performance potential. No one asked Amanda, "Why are you struggling?"

They were fixated on how she was exhibiting that struggle, not why. And that lit a fire in her to create a program that addressed the why. Not just what kids are doing that's getting them in trouble, but why they are suffering, and what in their life is creating chaos that then manifests into mental health disorders or addiction issues.

Dr. Amanda Shumow's Story

To give you some idea of my background, during my time in middle school through Sophomore year, I was a "if she applied herself" kind of student. During the second month of tenth grade, I was so depressed that I refused to go to school. I had been using drugs here and there, but the larger issue was that I was unmotivated and just didn't care. My parents hired a consultant who met with me, and after some testing they decided to send me to boarding school. No one ever asked if anything was bothering me or tried to get at any underlying issues.

My experience wasn't uncommon. I believe that schools give up on kids without trying to figure out what is causing the negative behavior. There is always a reason, but rarely do they try to figure it out. Once a kid is marked as "bad," this follows them. And this label can be applied as early as kindergarten. Just recently, my ten-year-old son's teacher (this kid likely has ADHD) sent an email telling me to tell him to "just try harder to focus."

A lack of education about learning disabilities creates a ripple in early education that affects the child's self-esteem, creates frustration, and then lack of desire to try. That's pretty much what happened to me. I got labeled, and I gave up. I started using at boarding school and then quit school altogether the summer before senior year. I then decided to do independent study.

> I went to treatment for the first time at 18 and thought it was a cult. Although I knew I had a problem, I had no interest in stopping. My parents drew a boundary and ended all financial support. Still, I used for the next two years. I ended up living in motels, and eventually I had no place to live. Then I got arrested and, long story short, I was sentenced to six to nine months of treatment.
>
> My inspiration to open Visions Adolescent Treatment Center was due to a lack of shorter-term, family inclusive programs in the country. I wanted to focus on creative, truly individualized programming catering to the holistic needs of the client and their families. The idea that the kid is the issue and should be sent away is wrong to me. It is the family system that should be challenged to change, not just the kid. We often see that the parents are sicker than the clients.
>
> I can't answer the question of what happens in treatment in a comprehensive way, since it really is different for every kid/family. A lot of factors change how long and at what degree a person needs support. These factors include: Assessment, diagnosis, medication management, treatment planning, teaching new tools, implementation of new tools, setback, family work, and school and peer stressors.
>
> At Visions, we aim for a year of support, but what that year looks like can be different for everyone. It may take one family 45 days to reach a "successful" session, and another two weeks. This is because success means different things to different families. A medication might be perfect for one kid who will report relief in a week, while one reports none in two, and we have to adjust.

While I'm highlighting Dr. Amanda Shumow's story and overall perspective, I do want to note that her outlook is very much aligned with the industry at large. I interact with counselors, therapists, psychologists, and psychiatrists on a daily basis at Visions, as well as through my private practice. I've met with literally hundreds over the last three years since I left the comprehensive setting. It's fair to say that these wishes Dr. Shumow addresses in the next section, especially, are very synchronous with the greater opinions that I've gathered throughout the last three years.

What Clinicians Wish Parents Knew

Mental health issues have always been present in substance abuse treatment, but ideas of how to treat mental health issues have become more developed and more acceptable to the masses. Parents would almost rather have a kid with mental health issues than a drug issue. When in fact, if someone is struggling with a THC addiction and mild depression, it is much easier to treat than someone who is using to combat OCD or bipolar disorder, for example. Beyond that:

- I wish parents understood that their kid doesn't want to do the things, or feel the way, they do.
- I wish that parents would not blame their kids for everything but truly look at and take responsibility for their part in the situation.
- I wish parents would set and hold reasonable boundaries and implement appropriate consequences, even when they don't want to.
- I wish parents would look at their kid and themselves in an honest way and know that we all have strengths and deficits in behavior—and that yes, it is their kid's fault sometimes. Not the teacher or system, or other kids—but yes, their kid.
- I wish parents would not do anything for a kid that the child is able to do for themselves. It is creating a generation of kids who don't believe they CAN do basic things.
- Please stop making excuses for your kid and for yourself.

What Clinicians Wish Schools Knew

What I wish schools knew depends on the age of the child. For instance, with little kids, early intervention works for learning disabilities and behavior issues. For older kids, it's important to understand that these kids are seeing more traumatic events and are exposed to so much more than we know. And it is having an effect on mood and behaviors. Even the kid that "looks" perfect is not.

But overall, offering counseling is a better option in lieu of suspension. Meditation and mindfulness instead of detention...and so on.

What Clinicians Wish Students Knew

- I wish students knew that we are on their side even if it doesn't seem like it all the time.
- Also, we could probably help if you were not afraid of us getting someone else in "trouble." While treatment can be highly structured, and it's easy to see us as an adversary or authority figure, we really are here to help. And the more we know, the better we can do that.
- We don't know it all. Treatment is a process and will evolve as we learn more about your family system, diagnosis, and your overall response.
- I wish students knew that not all clinicians ask how you feel all the time.

Do Your Research

One of the unexpected roles that I've assumed in my private practice is that people turn to me to help pair or identify a level of care, whether that be an individual therapist, even a tutor, all the way up to an inpatient residential treatment center. (We'll talk about levels of care in the next chapter.)

I've now done lots of research, visited lots of facilities, and observed prospective treatment options in action. What I've learned is that while a website might make a particular program look very cohesive, welcoming, and even well thought-out—the reality is that it's very important to do your research. It's very important to make sure that that facility is not just trained but *well-trained* in any treatment or programming that they offer. In other words, it's not a one-size-fits-all, and not everyone is created equal as far as treatment options are concerned.

Again, I'm not a clinician, but from an observational standpoint and working with lots of people in this field, I've seen that facilities often promote themselves based on what is currently popular. For example, a technique called brain spotting or brain mapping has been attracting clients. Different facilities will then start marketing that they offer brain spotting or brain mapping. And while they might offer that, the depth of training that's required to adequately serve a client and facilitate that process ethically and effectively is vast. While a facility might say that they offer it, and in fact they do, it doesn't mean that it's anywhere near the level of care that might be offered by another facility.

Dr. Amanda Shumow also notes issues with popular trends:

> Two trends I have seen recently are the various treatments of 'trauma' and the use of Dialectical Behavior Therapy (DBT). Clinicians become more versed in these modalities, and then programming gets developed to treat that demographic. For instance, six years ago we started using DBT, and we trained our whole staff. Now, programs are saying they do DBT just because they run a group once a week. It's the same with trauma. Programs say they treat trauma, but when you look into how and who, it's often lacking true experts. Modalities become selling points. I see the trend of using

a modality without proper training to sell a program, and I think it's dangerous.

Because it can be overwhelming to navigate all of this, one of the ways that parents commonly vet facilities is by using an educational consultant, or an "ed consultant," as they're called. Those professionals visit and vet those facilities. They go boots on the ground and see the whites of the eyes of the people who are running them.

But as a parent, it's possible to do independent research. This just requires asking questions like, "What is your training protocol? How many years of experience do you have in this field? What certifications and qualifications do you have?" Really making sure that there's a foundational level of support beneath any program offerings. Basically, you're checking the foundation to look for the integrity of the roof.

While you are always looking for a threshold of experience, that doesn't mean a clinician needs decades of experience, necessarily. A clinician could be new, and also very bright; they could be trained and mentored by an industry leader in that specific form of treatment. Age or years of experience is not always the bellwether, per se; however, I think looking at the full picture is effective.

To get the full picture, look at attrition rates and ask for references or referrals of parents and adolescents who have physically gone through the program. I think that's a great way to understand the quality.

But keep in mind, like Dr. Shumow stated earlier, every family is different, and every case is different. While your case might feel congruent to that of another family, even the slightest nuance can completely change a treatment progressive. Again, I'm not giving treatment. I'm not a clinician, and I'm not performing any therapy, so this is only from my perspective working in a treatment facility and interacting with many professionals that do.

Conclusion

If I could wave a wand, my wish would be that any student who ultimately is faced with a decision to exit their traditional, typical educational experience has been provided opportunity for rehabilitation, expression, and connection. And if they're leaving, it's not purely from a punitive standpoint where they were shown the door without being given any grace or any opportunity to really lay it on the table and find deeper meaning or root causes for their behavior.

While I'm talking in this chapter about one of the highest levels of care, the next chapter will center on the multiple levels of care. Imagine levels of care like a staircase of need, and we're going to look at each one. In the meantime, please visit www.recoveredu.com for the book study, supplement resources, and relevant links that accompany the content of this chapter.

CHAPTER EIGHT

Levels of Care

In this chapter I'm going to share strategies for educators, strategies for parents, and finally strategies students themselves can use as they move through the levels of care and the recovery process. But first we're going to build understanding of levels of care. This concept is used in any area of medicine for different levels of rehabilitation, from physical therapy all the way to mental health or substance recovery. This chapter is both for educators and parents to better understand what the levels of care mean and where they're most commonly applicable to students. It addresses when, how, and why a student might access a level of care, as well as congruency between the levels. Students might move either up through these levels or back down through them to their school or home setting.

In education we talk about having the least restrictive environment, or free appropriate placement. The goal with levels of care is also to provide students access to therapy and healing in the least restrictive environment. Typically, that means giving them access while they're still attending their normal school and living in their normal home setting. But it can also mean that students are no longer at home, or no longer at their school setting; they may be receiving services in isolation from their normal life.

Within this chapter, we will specifically detail each level of care. But as an overview before we begin, I want you to imagine the levels of care are just like a staircase. At the ground floor is a typical peer who's happy, healthy, and perhaps luckily void of any therapeutic needs. While the highest level, at the top of the stairs, is the most critical level of care. This is a hospitalization setting, which typically students enter through an emergency room. This serves as a temporary facility for safekeeping and stabilization before the appropriate level of care is identified.

Very commonly, children will traverse the stairs in sequential order, one at a time, working each level. They will then access a higher level of care if that level of care before it didn't yield results. But it's also not uncommon for a student to slingshot from the ground floor to the top floor, or anywhere in between, within their recovery process.

Levels of Care

Levels of care are complex. It seems like every day I'm still learning more about them. The work that I do now is in a setting that houses three levels of care at the same time. This means that different students are accessing three different levels of care in one setting. I work in an IOP and PHP. I also work with kids who are just coming in for therapy. IOP stands for intensive outpatient program. PHP is partial hospitalization program. Most people are familiar with therapy, to some degree, which is where we will start.

To help articulate the levels of care, and what their foundational purpose is, and the populations they best served, I called upon Dr. Fiona Ray to help me expand on that for my readers. Dr. Fiona Ray is the clinical director of an adolescent treatment program that provides multi-levels of care across the continuum of need. She's a person who has worked in the field with adolescents for well over 15 years. While I am going to guide us through the levels of care, this information is based on my conversations with her.

In the next section, I will touch upon what the levels of care are, who they're for, how they work, and their relationship with one another. It's important to note, however, that the nuances and program offerings of specific programs differ based on client needs and with specific professional settings; these descriptions are here to provide basic understanding and context.

Therapy

Therapy is the first level of care. With therapy, there are generally no long-term commitments. Perhaps the child will go alone, or with a parent. Maybe the whole family will go and speak to a therapy provider, such as a counselor, therapist, or psychologist. They will work on coping skills, such as how to deal with anxiety and depression. They'll help break down family dynamics and open up lines of communication. Generally, they work on sorting through the past, while building skills for the future.

Therapy is generally contained to that specific child, or to that specific family unit. Sessions are typically once per week, or once individually for the child and then perhaps later in the week with child and parent, if that's the particular situation. But generally, once to twice per week.

Outpatient/Intensive Outpatient (IOP)

An outpatient program is an elevated level of care and something that students often do in addition to individual therapy. Instead of it being an "either/or," it's typically an "and." The student might still have individual therapy, and then attend an outpatient program at least three times a week. As need grows, they may attend five times a week, increasing the threshold to that of an intensive outpatient program. Generally speaking, to be considered outpatient the services are delivered in three, three-hour increments per week, whereas an intensive outpatient program (IOP) is 15 hours per week.

In an OP/IOP setting, students are most likely working in small groups. They would be working on different skills, recovery techniques, or mental wellness techniques with other peers. These would be guided by a clinician or professional in that realm. In OP/IOP, students might have an hour of dialectical behavior therapy, or they might do an hour of trauma work, or meditation. They might do dramatic arts therapy, psychotherapy, or a combination therein. Those are just examples. But it is more of a program facilitated by a third person. It's not something that you just go to when you want to.

OP/IOP is generally a commitment of several weeks or several months. Programs are usually 3–6 p.m. or 4–7 p.m., with afternoon and/or evening session times intentionally available to students after the school day is over. Obviously, this time commitment can conflict with completing school assignments.

And again, if we're looking at the least restrictive environment for recovery or for therapeutic services, therapy and OP/IOP are both functions that allow the student to still go through their school day, live at home, have generally most of their day look very typical and feel very normal, while still receiving services.

Partial Hospitalization (PHP)

The next level of care above IOP is PHP, or a partial hospitalization program. A partial hospitalization would generally be from 8 a.m.–5 p.m., or similar hours, Monday through Friday. Up in west Los Angeles where I work, our students come every day and they're with us from 10 a.m.–7 p.m. PHP programs must meet a minimum of six hours per day to meet this classification.

With PHP, students are no longer being educated in their traditional comprehensive environment. In fact, they're having school hours in a small setting on the same site where they are receiving individual therapy and group therapy. Essentially, PHP combines the elements of school, therapy, and IOP into one.

It's a comprehensive program Monday through Friday. Still though, students are typically living at home, or perhaps in an extended care facility or a sober living facility. But they are generally in their same zip code, in their same community, and most often sleeping in their own bed at night.

Residential Treatment Center (RTC)

Above a PHP is an RTC, which is a residential treatment center. When I was a kid and people talked about "going to rehab," this is generally what they were referring to. With RTC, students are living at a facility with 24-hour care.

The emphasis on education at this level has been significantly reduced. Typically, in a residential treatment program students are really only doing about two hours of school a day. Whereas in a PHP program, education and therapeutic needs are parallel in their emphases; half of the time they're doing school, and half of the time they're doing therapeutic activities.

With RTC, they're no longer living at home. They no longer have access to the outside world, really. It's more of a confined environment that lends itself to healing and recovery. And depending on where you go, and whether you're working with your insurance or private pay, the scope and length can be different.

Many of the programs that I'm most familiar with have a 45-day minimum stay, although it's not uncommon for kids to be there longer. The length of stay is really determined by the student's progress, their ability to heal and to develop coping skills that will sustain them once they leave. But RTCs typically have a threshold, or a maximum length of stay. If a student is progressing as they should, and after this maximum length of stay, the student is unable or unwilling for any reason to return to their home environment, they might be offered a long-term residential setting. This is commonly referred to as a therapeutic boarding school.

RTC programs will look different, and they'll serve niche populations. There are specific centers that might treat eating difficulties. There are ones that are primary mental health focused. There are ones that focus on dual diagnosis, so they're treating elevated substance use, perhaps alcoholism or drug use, at the same time as they're addressing mental health needs. As you get into the space of residential treatment centers, they become more specified in what they treat, and how they treat it.

Extended Care

Extended Care (EC) facilities are a midway point between RTC and home. In many cases, students live in an EC while attending an OP/IOP or PHP. The length of stay can vary based on provider, but a 90-day minimum stay is a safe estimate as a baseline. The function of EC is for students to work back toward certain typical privileges and access to more typical elements of adolescent life. As students live within the EC environment, these touchstones are delivered via the clinical and structured setting, thus removing the power struggle of these integrations from the home setting. Common examples include:

- Device management.
- Identifying and establishing healthy peer groups.
- Demonstrating commitment to on-going support such as peer support groups.
- Adhering to curfew.
- Employment or educational frameworks.

Extended Care is a place to beta test recovery and assess if the student is indeed ready to return home, or whether they need to perhaps explore longer-term care such as a therapeutic board school.

Therapeutic Boarding School

A therapeutic boarding school, which I briefly mentioned above, is often a longer-term solution beyond the PHP, RTC and EC settings.

It can be more academic-driven, more typical in access to common activities like athletic teams and school events. But it's under 24-hour care in a more confined environment. Confined in the sense of less access to technology, to the outside world, and certainly to drugs and alcohol. Students might finish their high school career there and go on to college.

Therapeutic boarding schools are accredited institutions that do prepare students for the next level of education, or to enter the workforce if that's their goal. When a student goes to a therapeutic boarding school, that's not always a tell that they couldn't succeed elsewhere. It's just that that was the best level of care for their long-term health and their long-term goals, as well as the family's long-term plan for that child. It is common that a family who places their child at an RTC is seeking a higher level of containment than can be achieved in the home setting.

Hospitalization Hold

Above residential would be a hospitalization. And this is what I meant when I said you could slingshot from the ground floor to the top floor. For example, if a student is living at home and has never expressed any outward signs or symptoms to a parent and then, perhaps, is having active or passive suicide ideation, or even a suicide attempt, that student would be hospitalized, typically through an emergency room.

The hospitalization would commonly last for a minimum of 72 hours and could be referred to as a 5150 hold. During this time, the child is heavily evaluated by a mental health team, including psychologists, psychiatrists, and social workers. They talk to the family and collect information. With a hospitalization, the primary goal is to keep the child safe and alive, while also providing some time and space for deciding what the next step should be.

In that 72-hour hold, the clinical team will give their recommendations about which level of care is best suited for that need.

That student is now at the top of the staircase. Maybe that means they do go to residential, or maybe they can go to a PHP. Maybe they go to an OP/IOP, or maybe they just need to go to therapy. It really just depends on the recommendations from those professionals as to the specific safety and therapeutic treatment plan for the child. The resources, such as funds and insurance, all play in as well. Here, students are at the most elevated level of care, with the shortest duration, generally as a holding tank and a safety net to then assess the next steps for a treatment plan for that student.

Strategies for Educators

Now that you are more familiar with the different levels of care, it's also important to discuss specific strategies that can help relevant stakeholders coordinate with clinicians.

The following strategies are ones that I have been trained in, and currently work with every day in my professional setting. These strategies are derived from serving on student support teams, IEP teams, 504 teams, and from working through release of information with therapists, doctors, councilors, and treatment center providers. Again, as the education and curriculum specialist for a mental health and wellness high school, my job day in and day out is to facilitate communication between schools, parents, teachers, and families so that everybody is on the same page. The goal is to yield the best results for that individual student.

An educator is best positioned to tangibly deliver education to their student when they are well educated themselves on not only the specifics regarding that student, but they also have a good grasp on what that level of care contains. Which brings us to the first strategy.

Ask questions

While it seems fairly obvious, the best point of entry for an educator is to ask questions in order to garner as much information as possible.

Of course, this is while remaining mindful of stepping over a boundary that a family doesn't want crossed. But essentially, educators can politely and assertively invite themselves into that student's particular case, so to best understand how to support them.

I remember as a teacher, and even as an assistant principal, having so many questions I wanted to ask families. For instance, "Do you have an advocate, or somebody who is communicating on behalf of the family?" But I felt afraid to ask questions because it was all so deeply personal. I didn't want to offend them. I didn't know if I should ask, or if I could.

But the bottom line is, there's nothing wrong with asking questions. If a family doesn't feel comfortable sharing information, they won't. They'll tell you that they won't. But what I've learned from working closely with parents now, is that oftentimes the lack of questions from educators sends a message to the family that the educator is uninterested or lacks sympathy for that family.

When educators ask questions and go all in with a family, it builds trust. It provides a sense of relief and validation for that student and the parents when they feel that the teacher really wants information and will use it according to what is best for that child.

Of course, this doesn't mean that an educator needs to do whatever the family is asking them to do. Everyone has boundaries, structure, and protocol within their school site, on their team, or in their district. But asking for information changes the tone. It elevates the level of collaboration and communication. And above all, it yields results that you can't get if you don't ask the questions.

Keep in mind that too many questions may be off-putting to families. Too many questions or not enough questions can both result in a lack of communication, which results in a lack of progress. Even if you're choosing your questions wisely, make sure you also choose an appropriate tact and tone.

As a teacher, if you're struggling with how to ask a question, the answer's in the building. A school psychologist or counselor is a good resource to help you with the semantics of asking a question. But, as a general guide: As opposed to a tone of, "What's wrong with your child?" you'd be better served with something like, "I understand that your child is going through some things. It appears that they're struggling, and I just want you to know that I would love to support you. To do that, it would help to have more specific, tangible information that would give me a better avenue to provide that support."

In other words, take a tone of compassion. "I care for your child, and I'd love to help you. The more information you feel comfortable providing, the more I can specifically support your needs."

In addition, the concept of accommodations is generally very checkboxy. If this... do this... But in asking and receiving information from a family, you can really individualize those accommodations. You can apply grace more willingly and with more confidence since it is backed by tangible information. Whether it is the extension of deadlines, or dismissing previous assignments, the information can inform the accommodations to that specific student.

Get a Release of Information (ROI), when possible

Once you have asked questions and opened a dialogue, get a Release of Information, if possible. We talked about the Release of Information (ROI) in chapter four. But again, just briefly, I will stress how helpful this document can be. An ROI is a document that can be signed by the family; a teacher; and the doctor, counselor, or therapist. This way all three parties can openly share information. Teachers are used to filling out paperwork. If a student is trying to get an IEP or a 504 plan, a teacher will be asked to give observations about their behavior, their performance, their attendance, and their affect within the classroom setting.

But with the release of information, the information is being exchanged each way. The teacher can then have access to more information specific to that student case, and better understand and support the specific diagnoses. The teacher and the therapist can talk on the phone or via email, all in the effort to better support that student and that family in the process of recovery.

Strategies for Parents

The parent piece is often more complex, more emotional, and more sensitive. Whereas a teacher might have 100+ students on their role sheet, as a parent you might have just one child, or maybe two or three children. So instead of it being one one-hundredth of your focus, it's 100% of your focus, or a great deal.

Deliver as Much Tangle Information to the School as Possible

When I work with parents now, and they're feeling frustrated with lack of progress in the school setting, or they're just overwhelmed with where to start—I always encourage them to deliver as much information to the school as possible.

Sometimes it feels impossible to deliver transparency. And I'm not saying that you must ship all the medical records to every teacher. But a letter from your child's clinician, or therapist, or doctor, can go a long way towards educating the teachers, the counselor, or other school site stakeholders on the specific diagnosis. Make sure the letter includes:

- What are the symptoms of the diagnosis?
- How is it most likely to manifest in school?
- What kinds of things can educators do to best support that specific student?

Tangible information goes beyond just saying your child isn't feeling well, or they're feeling quite anxious. When possible, deliver information that's substantive and validated by a professional. This will encourage and expand the support that as a parent you are likely craving.

Identify Your Point Person

When I work with parents, I see how challenging it can be for them. When you're managing a very volatile, emotional, and overall scary time at home, you don't have free time to email all six teachers, the counselor, the principal, and so on. Or to call or meet with them.

So, as I've said in previous chapters, try to work with the school site to identify one point-person; this someone will be the communication conduit between the family and the school site. And oftentimes, most traditionally, that would be the school's counselor. So that is a logical place to start. It could also be the teacher that you have the best relationship with, which is probably also the teacher that you trust the most. If you disseminate information through that point person, then that point person can share it with the larger team.

Strategically, pick the path of least resistance emotionally for you. When we get overwhelmed, oftentimes we do nothing. And if emailing everyone is overwhelming, email only your point person. Focus on this one place to start to bridge that communication and ensure that information is getting through. If you can begin to ease some of your own anxiety in this way, it gets the ball rolling towards results.

Strategies for Students

We live in a time where there's a lot of pushback about over-parenting, helicopter parenting, or snowplow parenting—where parents are running every aspect of the student's life and distributing all information. So, whether it's at a 504 meeting, or another meeting where all stakeholders come to the table together, where and when possible, if the student can communicate through their own words and be vulnerable, it shifts the entire dynamic.

Include the Student's Voice

The power of the student voice is undeniable. Especially in high school, educators are eager to hear information from the student themselves. Obviously, the comfort level for each child will be different with this. I work with students who are super confident in delivering information about their mental health or recovery. I also have students who are overwhelmed with the situation, and therefore unable to communicate effectively.

Communication can be as simple as a letter that somebody else reads or gives to the teachers or staff. Because if a student can verbalize in any capacity how they're feeling and what that struggle looks like, it makes the whole situation more tangibly human.

Educators are in education because they love kids, and they want to support them. When a child is able to deliver even just a drop of vulnerability by delivering information in their own words, I've seen teachers and schools go to great lengths to support that child.

And while the student voice is incredibly impactful, I'm also quick to note that using it is not always possible. You may want to talk to their clinician or doctor about it first. Would sitting in a meeting or writing this letter create more damage than positive results? It's not about forcing them to communicate. It's about empowering them to communicate. It's about having them step into that moment and understand that it's okay to not be okay, and it's okay to verbalize their needs to those who are in a position to help them.

When a parent is the one to make the demands and raise the concerns—and the student doesn't say a word—educators may suspect a song and dance, perhaps to get a student out of academic trouble. We live in a time where parent access to information has amped up college admissions pressures to create a frenzy. And that frenzy has created a defensive posturing response from a lot of educators.

When they get an email from a parent, for example, they sometimes hesitate to open it because they don't know if you're going to come at them high and to the right. Whereas the student voice can disarm, legitimize, and coordinate all stakeholders. And again, if the student can say it out loud, great. But even having them write a letter that somebody could read, or sending an email, is effective every time.

Conclusion

Information is power. It allows you to make the best decisions and to move with intention, integrity, and empathy. Common to many chapters in this book, I think the theme here is information, understanding, and transparency. The purpose of this chapter is to get all of the stakeholders to share information, to collaborate, and coordinate as a united front. It's also for educators, students, and parents to all understand the levels of care and how they interrelate with one another.

When a student hits a PHP or residential level, that is often where the most roadblocks start to occur with a student's ability to maintain their footprint academically in a school where they're not physically present. A large majority of my job, both in my private practice and working with the day school up in Los Angeles, is made up of communicating and fostering channels of communication. The goal is for students to continue to complete their work that they would be doing at their comprehensive school, while they're receiving treatment within the continuum of care.

I spend a lot of time informing educators on what the PHP or residential level of care is, why it's crucial for students' recovery and success, and how usually the goal is for the student to return to their home and to their school. Often, for an educator or teacher, it's out of sight, out of mind. "Well, the student's not physically in my classroom. Why is it even in the interests of the student for me to coordinate and allow them to work remotely?" But with so many other parts of their life changing, holding onto and maintaining continuity where they can is really important.

And even more than that, these students are there for medical reasons. They're not on a vacation. I often find myself asking reluctant educators if they would be posturing the same way if that same student was undergoing a robust treatment for cancer. I know that sounds harsh, but really, they're both medically needed, and they need to be treated accordingly.

We now have have a better understanding of communication protocol, suggestions, and strategies, in addition to the various levels of care that are in play within a student's recovery process. In the next chapter, I want to shift gears and look at some different progressive programs and partners that are available to schools and families, both in high school and as students enter college . In the meantime, please visit www.recoveredu.com for the book study, supplement resources, and relevant links that accompany the content of this chapter.

CHAPTER NINE

Progressive Programs and Partners

Throughout this book, we have been examining how educators and parents can support student mental health and recovery. Now, I would like to highlight a few key movements, legislative acts, and specific programs throughout the country that are leading by example to address student needs in ways that are innovative and affect change.

As a teacher and as an administrator, I've come to understand that the answer is always in the room. It's one of my favorite sayings. Because when you have a dilemma within a classroom, a school, or the larger school district, the answer is always in the room. If we imagine that our room is the United States educational system, there are different players that have activated solutions already in a micro sense. We can use these as examples to create change on a macro level.

There are hundreds of examples that I could draw from, but I've chosen a few that speak to me for different reasons. These are examples that I think will help us drive the conversation further as we continue to work together towards more effective solutions for our students in the mental health and substance realm.

In the programs that we're going to review together, mental health or substance abuse isn't an afterthought. It's the forethought. These programs accept the reality that without wellness from a mental health perspective, learning can't happen effectively. They are all forward thinking and proactive in their approach to addressing these concerns. We will look at high school programs, as well as college level programs.

We haven't spoken much about the college perspective in this book, but for many of our learners, it's the logical next step in their journey. I want to bring in some college programs so that we as educators are aware of the resources that are available at the next level; this context will provide better perspective when working with a student who is struggling or has a very high support system in high school. We should not be limited by thinking such as, "Well, we can't do all of these things for them in high school because that level of support is not available in the 'real world' or in college." I've heard this line of reasoning from plenty of educators.

Because, contrary to that assumption, a lot of colleges do have programs offering that level of support. There are places and programs on college campuses that assist with mental health and recovery. So when a student is well, functioning with autonomy, and ready to go to the college setting, they can look for schools that have wraparound services or different levels of care within the larger campus community.

Recent Legislation

More recently, a few states are now taking the topic of mental health awareness from a conversation to the implementation phase with public policy and law. For example, in Oregon a student-driven initiative has resulted in excused mental health days.

You might think, well, people have always been able to just take a day off. But previously what parents would do was say that their child was sick. They would claim a traditional illness, like the stomach flu, when in reality that student was sad, anxious, or overwhelmed and just needed a break. So now, it's in an effort to reduce the stigma that we've talked about over and over again, they're empowered to write, "mental health day" as an excuse.

Mental health is part of our whole health. And instead of shading it under the guise of something else, like the stomach flu, now it's an accepted absence. It's parallel to a traditional illness, as we would traditionally think of it in the school setting. The law itself gives students five mental health days in a three-month period. So, they wouldn't even need a parent's note. It's part of a larger movement overall, and sometimes the messaging is just as important, if not more important, than the law itself.

Florida is also making strides in its commitment to deliver mental health awareness through education to students. In 2018, they implemented a policy where, starting in sixth grade all the way through high school, students would receive at least five hours of mental health education per year. That might not sound like much, but consider that in a lot of schools, mental health education is zero, unless you take a psychology class, maybe. And five hours annually, over seven years, means that by the time they graduate high school, they'll have had 35 hours of mental health education.

Imagine the conversations these students would be able to have as seniors in high school if they started learning about mental health as a sixth grader! That self-awareness and empowerment to really command their own advocacy—to not just survive adolescence, but thrive into adulthood.

And most recently, Governor Gavin Newsom of California signed into legislation a law that prevents schools from suspending disruptive students. This was controversial, and the jury is still out, so to speak, on its effectiveness. But for me, this is really in line with the restorative justice model, of which I am a huge advocate. With this legislation, Newsom is recognizing the reality that many of our most disruptive students are demonstrating behaviors as manifestations of other ailments such as a learning disability, a mental health condition, being bullied, feeling isolated, living in poverty, or dealing with daily discrimination or racial profiling.

If you remember from chapter two, restorative justice looks for alternative means of correction, or alternative ways to deliver a consequence for students. It provides them with an opportunity to reflect on, learn from, and gain traction from their mistakes. This way, they can course correct and change their trajectory within the school setting.

So what Governor Newsom is doing is asking the schools to re-examine the way they address issues with students who are showing symptoms of larger problems. I firmly agree that we need to really limit, if not eliminate, the practice of outsourcing our children. By "outsourcing," I mean that if they don't fit into the comprehensive box of a typical peer, then they must go somewhere else or be somewhere else—out of sight, out of mind.

With this legislation, Oregon, Florida, and California are formalizing the conversation. I've said before that we have to formalize to normalize. If we want our students and educators to be empowered to address mental health and think creatively and innovatively, then we need to formalize this legislatively like these states are doing. And we need to do that collectively. All 50 states should have legislation and supports in place that allow for mental health and overall recovery to parallel other factors within education.

THE GEFFEN ACADEMY

One of the educational programs that I'm really inspired by is the Geffen Academy, which is a middle and high school housed on the UCLA campus in Los Angeles. The Geffen Academy is a public-private hybrid. It's a private school with tuition, but it also has public funding for research and to offset the cost of tuition for over 30% of the students who attend. This financial assistance is intended to drive diversity, both racially and economically.

The wellness director of that school is Ross Szabo, a social innovator who pioneered the youth mental health movement. At age 16, Ross was diagnosed as having bipolar disorder with anger control problems and psychotic features. He turned this diagnosis into an opportunity to educate others. His natural ability to make mental health approachable for large groups of people has led to countless media appearances.

Ross Szabo is also an award-winning speaker, author and the CEO of Human Power Project, a company that designs mental health curriculum. He wanted to be a part of Geffen Academy because he knew they could create a replicable program that teaches mental health. In this way, their program can function as a model for other schools around the world.

I had the privilege of watching a keynote speech by Ross highlighting his struggle with bipolar disorder and discussing a curriculum that he has developed for schools to foster students' understanding of their own mental wellness. Quite frequently, when we talk about mental health, we do so in a reactive and negative connotation. We have adopted a posture where we infer students only have mental health if something's wrong with them, and then the rest of the time, "They don't have mental health." When in reality, mental health is a spectrum, as Ross Szabo describes in the next section.

Ross Szabo's Spectrum of Mental Health

Everyone has mental health, and Ross has developed a spectrum that relates this. It's about identifying where on that spectrum you are. At the high end of the spectrum is someone able to balance, and at the opposite end is someone who is not able to balance. Then there are gradations between. Someone might move through the entire spectrum on a daily basis, weekly, monthly, yearly, or perhaps throughout a decade. And it can be an ebb and flow.

In Ross's own words:

> The premise for rethinking the mental health spectrum is that most people currently think of mental health in a way that is harmful. When most people hear of a mental health spectrum, they think: On one side

you have people who are sane or who don't have any issues, in the middle you have people with mild mental health disorders, and on the far end there are people with severe mental health disorders.

There are two things wrong with this spectrum. The first thing is that you can have a severe mental health disorder and be sane at the same time. If you are on two places of the spectrum at the same time, then something is wrong with the spectrum. The other difficult thing about the current spectrum is that it promotes the concept that only people with severe disorders need help and everyone else is okay.

If this thinking were applied to a physical health spectrum, then the equivalent messaging we would receive is you don't need to exercise until you get cancer. You don't need to eat healthily until you get diabetes. With physical health, we are proactive and preventative. With mental health, we are reactive and judgmental.

So we need a different spectrum. The spectrum needs to be more like physical health in order to normalize mental health and be inclusive of everyone. The spectrum that I use has five places on it.

- Able to Balance
- Difficult to Balance
- Need Help to Balance
- Need Constant Assistance to Balance
- Unable to Balance

Able to balance is someone who doesn't have to think about their mental health much. They don't have a lot of stress or triggers or trauma. They kind of float through life without considering what they need to address. Much like there are people who don't need to work out or eat healthy to be thin, there are people who don't work on their mental health to stay balanced.

Difficult to balance is when someone is aware they have stress and triggers, and that they need to cope, but they aren't actively taking steps to address those challenges. It's the equivalent of someone who knows they should eat healthy and should exercise to take care of their physical health, but instead chooses to eat some doughnuts and not do anything physically active.

Need Help to Balance is someone who may be in therapy or on medication, however it can also be someone who knows that they need to listen to music, talk to a friend, go for a walk, exercise, play a game or do something in order to help balance their mental health. You don't need to have a physical health disorder to work on your physical health, and you don't need to have a mental health disorder to work on your mental health. Needing help to balance mental health is something that a majority of us need.

Need Constant Assistance to Balance could be someone in an outpatient program, AA or NA; however, it can also be someone who went through something so difficult that they need constant assistance. We see this often when a friend or family member experiences some type of loss. We take it upon ourselves to make sure they aren't alone. We sleep on their couch, we cook for them, and we take care of them until we are certain they can be alone again.

Unable to Balance could be someone who is suicidal, but it could also be someone who went through something so difficult that no matter what they try they aren't able to balance their mental health. Being unable to balance has nothing to do with functioning. When my dad died I wasn't able to balance my mental health for months. It didn't matter if I had constant support; it didn't matter if I used a coping mechanism. The grief of losing my dad was so strong that nothing allowed me to balance. I still functioned. I went to school every day; I taught every day; I was in a master's program, and I maintained relationships, but I couldn't balance my mental health.

Ross Szabo talks more about this in his book, *Behind Happy Faces*, which you should all pick up. What I love about his spectrum is that it helps us understand that mental health is a fluid process. It's going to change. And as it changes, the levels of care we need, the support we need, and the resources that we need also change. The spectrum facilitates a conversation around where we find ourselves today versus yesterday, versus where we want to see ourselves tomorrow. What resources do we need to move toward the "able to balance" end of the spectrum?

What Makes the Geffen Academy Unique

The Geffen Academy is a school that prides itself on rigor, but it also prides itself on addressing the concept of the whole child. And the reason that this program is so important is that built into their school day are not only traditional courses and modes of inquiry, but a focus on intellectual curiosity and awakening a passion for learning.

In contrast to a traditional school that has a very standard curriculum resulting in students feeling lost in that shuffle, students at the Geffen Academy are granted an opportunity to conduct an immense amount of individualized and self-identified research projects from sixth through twelfth grade.

Within their school day, students have an advisory period that is all about wellness. They learn about getting enough sleep, their relationship with technology, their relationship with their peers, and how to communicate with their family. They also learn about drugs, alcohol, sex, peer pressure—all of the topics that generally aren't addressed very often in school. Instead of addressing these issues briefly in a standalone one-semester health class, this learning occurs every day throughout their entire career.

In Ross's words, this is what differentiates Geffen Academy from a comprehensive/traditional school:

> In terms of my work, students at Geffen Academy have a class where they learn about their mental health and the impact it has in their

lives once a week from grades 6-12. We feel it is important to have this type of consistency during adolescent development in order to match the types of skills students need with the changes they are experiencing. Another thing that is different is that students learn from educators who have lived experience with mental health disorders and developmental disabilities. Studies show that the most effective way to lessen stigma surrounding these issues is to have contact with a person who has a diagnosis. It's an essential part of normalizing mental health in our school community.

You can say that you want mental health to have equal footing with rigorous academics, but the proof is in the pudding. At Geffen Academy, it's no longer just a talking point. It's a tangible touchstone to their commitment to student wellness and mental health.

According to Ross, students leave the Geffen Academy with these fundamental tools and coping strategies:

- A clear definition that mental health is the same as physical health.
- Vocabulary to discuss mental health challenges.
- Mindfulness.
- Neuroscience exercises to utilize good stress in their lives.
- A clear differentiation between effective/ineffective coping strategies.
- Steps for human behavior change.
- Affirmative consent lessons.
- Steps to create healthy relationships.
- Life skills for financial literacy, self-defense, cooking, sewing, and changing a tire.
- Knowing the role that risk-taking plays in adolescent development.
- Knowing the impact of brain development on adolescent development.

The Diamond Bar Peer Counseling Program

Another model that I consider to be very important and progressive is the comprehensive peer counseling program at Diamond Bar High School. This program has been in motion for years now and operates as an electives class in which kids get ongoing training and facilitation experience. They plan their messaging and work on their caseloads, but they also have a stand alone peer-to-peer counseling model for students to drop in for support.

Those students are trained and monitored by high level professionals in the field. And again, this is a peer-to-peer model where students can address their issues with normal things that are going on that perhaps don't require clinical care. But it's a place for them to interact with highly trained peers that can help guide them, give them tools, and be a listening ear.

Diamond Bar is not the first peer-to-peer counseling model, but I would say that they are one of the most successful and sustainable models that I have discovered. Peer counselors apply, interview, and train. They are then in a class together, as part of their day. It's not an ancillary club. Again, this is a great example of a successful peer-to-peer model for schools looking to implement something similar.

Diamond Bar has also opened a comprehensive wellness center on their school campus that addresses the whole student and the classic dimensions of wellness. Not just academic wellness, but physical wellness, occupational wellness, intellectual wellness, cultural wellness, social wellness, emotional wellness, and spiritual wellness. They have what they call "wellness consultants," who are trained students facilitating that program, under the leadership of the staff wellness team of educators and professionals. They even have things like therapy dogs that they bring in once a week.

Haven at College

Recently, I was invited to speak on a college campus at a very large, well known public university. When I arrived to talk, I delivered my story of mental health and substance troubles in college. I then spoke about the coping skills, tools, and resources that are available to students.

What I discovered from the many students that contacted me after I spoke, was that they either didn't know how to access the supports that were available to them on college campuses or they didn't feel that the supports on the college campus were authentic or confidential. There was also an issue with turnaround time, or the inundation of the need versus the resources available. They had to wait several weeks just to get an appointment. They then became submerged in the daily college obligations and did not end up seeing anyone at all.

This is not uncommon. Based on size, stemming from the rising mental health and substance crisis that's happening in college campuses right now, school resources are overwhelmed. A particular program that I believe is vital, innovative, and successful in filling in these gaps is Haven at College.

Haven at College is positioned on many college campuses around the United States, and it's growing quickly. At its core, it provides housing. It provides all the levels of care, essentially, from therapy to peer-to-peer mentorship to sober living. Through Haven at College, there is a sense of community, accountability, and support for mental health, substance, or concurring dual diagnosis needs. And it's available to students at a variety of campuses so that they can go to college and have the college experience, but they can do it with structure in place. This allows them to persevere through their mental health or recovery needs.

The Haven at College program is located at USC, University of San Francisco, Cal Poly, UC Santa Barbara, University of Redlands, University of Maryland, Tufts, Miami University, Oxford, and Drexel in Pennsylvania. I think the reason that it's so successful is that it operates on that core philosophy of peer-to-peer. Of course, this is within a larger organization of guidance and professional management by a clinical staff and adults who have a high level of training and experience in the field. So it is built to move with the ebb and flow of student needs and provide higher-level care, like a sober dorm with 24/7 supervision, or just an individualized program or individualized mentorship program. There is a big spectrum within those options to fit the needs of the students at those schools.

Haven at College program is a great is a great example of where a high level of support can exist and does so in a supportive way. It won't interfere with the education or the college experience, but it will help the student remain healthy and able to achieve their goals within a larger school setting that is inundated with temptation, peer pressure, and everybody living at a very fast pace.

Jordan Porco Foundation (JPF)

The final program that I really want to focus on is the Jordan Porco Foundation, the JPF. They are a foundation that serves to provide resources, education, and decrease stigma with mental health both in high school and the college setting.

The highlight of their programming is what they call Fresh Check Day. It's essentially a formalized version of what I did when I was on that college campus late last year. On campus, I met with students, and I helped them better understand the resources that were available to them, either within their university student services, or through private channels in the greater community. While the original intent of my visit was different, the vast need on campus was too large to disregard or delay connecting students to resources. The greatest takeaway for me on this visit was that we forget that college students, especially ones who had not struggled in earlier adolescence, may not know the logical or sequential steps to find and receive help.

For Fresh Check Day, JPF arrives at a college campus, having already coordinated with the school that they're visiting to set up tables and drive PR campaigns. This way, students are aware of the various supports in place on their campus, how to access them, what they're for, who they're for, and why it's relevant to them. This might be connecting them to the student wellness options on campus, student support organizations, or even other peers facing similar roadblocks.

Essentially, members of JPF check in with the students and see how they're doing. They also, in a very casual, energetic, and empathetic way, point them in a very clear direction to resources. This takes away the confusion and the stigma involved with feeling like you can hardly catch your breath on a college campus, let alone take the time to figure out who you need to see, where they are, and when you can see them. Let's not forget for most students this is the first time they are living on their own, managing their own lives, and balancing the obligations of being a student and peer.

The other thing to add about JPF is that in addition to pointing students in the right directions for their own needs, they're also very diligent in educating peers on what signs and signals to look for in their friends, their classmates, their dorm mates, or within their fraternity or sorority. Specifically signs and symptoms of suicide ideation, or other mental health concern. So essentially empowering them and arming them with information so that when they see something, they can say something.

The JPF has a lot of great resources for educators, schools, and parents on their website. In the age of Internet information overload, their site is cohesive, intuitive, and the perfect place to begin building your foundational knowledge of signs, symptoms and resources. You should check them out.

Conclusion

All of these programs serve as great examples of what is being done on high school and college campuses throughout the country, and what can be done still. And given the systemic, bureaucratic, and cultural roadblocks that a lot of educators and communities face, these programs have all found ways to traverse that landscape and still make a positive impact through progressive programming. They've partnered with students and educators to create a sense of community that elevates a level of support and awareness in terms of mental health and recovery issues for students and all stakeholders, really.

Like I said, there are there many, many examples. These are just a few, but they're all great places to start if you're looking to make a change, for a model to emulate, or for somebody to talk to. How were you able to start this program or what impact has it had? These are all people who are advocates for change, who are walking the walk, not just talking the talk.

So if you find yourself just talking and you want to start walking, I would look on their websites, follow them on Instagram, and start reading their blog posts. Then you can better understand how they're able to take concepts, pin them down on paper, and activate them into tangible systems on school campuses and college campuses.

For more information on these programs, in additional to any other programs referenced, please visit recover.edu for links and contact info. As you move to the conclusion of this book, I'll be going back over some thinking and talking points. Also, remember that there is a comprehensive book study available if you're ready to take your commitment to change to the next level. The book study comes complete with an overview of each chapter, relevant PDFs and handouts, and additional resources. The next and final chapter will include more details.

Conclusion: Communication not Isolation

The core tenet of this book is communication not isolation. Communication, as we've discussed, looks and feels different for every stakeholder. So can isolation. Sometimes we isolate out of an abundance of caution. For example, as an educator we don't ask questions for fear that we might offend or overstep boundaries. As a student or family, we might withhold information that we should be giving to the school because we're feeling shameful, guarded, or simply overwhelmed.

It is only when we finally break down those barriers keeping us isolated that we really start the process of collaboration and healing for our students. Now, this isn't to say that anyone needs to know *everything* about anyone else. But it is about communicating those vital pieces of information, as well as the strategies that will allow us to provide more support for students struggling with mental health and recovery from substance abuse.

I felt called to write this book because the work that inspires me the most is helping kids that other people have given up on. I've witnessed such incredible change, regrowth and healing in the work that I've done privately, in the comprehensive school setting, and now in the recovery school setting. Enough so that it makes me believe that a lot of those students wouldn't have gotten to that highest threshold of suffering, depression, or addiction had there been more eyes on them, and more systems in place to triage.

Adults are sometimes so overwhelmed by the dynamics of a student's struggle that they turn away, assuming a posture of, "See no evil, hear no evil." My goal is to promote more of a preventative approach, whereas historically, a reactive approach has been more common in education.

As you know, my passion for this issue comes from the fact that I am a person in recovery. That took me a long time to be able to say. First, I had to admit to myself that there was something that I needed to recover from, then I had to take the next step of admitting it to the ones that I loved and cared about. Only then did I have the courage to face those demons and lean into those issues through therapy and other treatment protocol. Finally, I've converted that experience into messaging with audiences throughout the country. With this, I hope to reach others who are struggling. I want to encourage them to lean in and face their issues, too.

Recovery is a polarizing word, and that fear of judgment stops people from seeking help or admitting that their children need help. It's essential for us to reframe our concept because we're all recovering from something. These things may be somewhat insignificant, but they also include the highest threshold of conflict and pain, of heartbreak and heartache, of loss and suffering. It's essential that we all begin to see recovery as a spectrum.

The Power of the Student Voice

I elected to lead this book with the student perspective because the student voice is powerful. As I've stated in the book, it only takes one adult to change the trajectory of a child's life. But as an educator I've discovered that more times than not, for me, it's been the opposite. My experience supporting Kaley as an assistant principal was me performing the work that I would ultimately fall in love with and do now professionally on a daily basis.

When I think of distinct changes in my philosophy, the tools that I employ, and the skills that I have obtained over time—they can all be traced back to a student who impacted me. A student whose story, struggle, and vulnerability either opened my eyes and allowed me to see avenues to support them or ways that I personally could do greater things. So, with Kaley I understood that not only could an adult affect powerful and lasting change on a student, but that a student also has that same ability to impact the educators in their life.

In reflecting on the student voice in chapter one, I want to encourage you as a reader to reflect on the ways that you are able to see, or not see, your students. What voice are you giving them? How are you empowering them? What channels do you create that positively enable vulnerability so that solutions can be reached and support can be given early and often?

Chapter two examines the concept of autonomy in terms of empowering an educator or anybody in the life of a child to think creatively through different methods, resources, and channels through which they can support that child. There's a lot of policy in education, and all of that serves its purpose from a systemic point of view. But, as somebody supporting a preteen or teenager in their journey, it's of the utmost importance to look for the gray area in an otherwise black-white scale. Look for creative solutions, knowing that even a small amount of grace for a student in need could dovetail into a significant amount of healing and change for that individual.

Parents in Crisis

Chapter three shifts to the parent perspective. In education, the parent perspective can be complicated, even under typical circumstances. There is a significant movement to encourage students, especially in middle school and high school, to have more independence. That is, for them not to be constantly under the thumb of a helicopter parent or a tiger mom—or whatever negative stereotype you'd prefer. But it's critical to shift to an opposite mindset when dealing with parents of a student in crisis.

These parents are very emotional, and oftentimes overwhelmed. This may be a life or death situation for their child. This is why it's so important to find ways to reach out and assert yourself as a partner. And when collaborating with them, issue as much compassion and empathy as you can. Empathy should take the form of tangible grace, loopholes, extensions, solutions—anything that can be given to that family to put your money where your mouth is.

A lot of times, as educators we will say that we understand mental health crises, or we say that we are familiar with addiction. We can talk all day long, but it's not until we physically and emotionally partner with those parents and those families that the meaning of our words takes shape and is validated.

Patrick's story is particularly heartbreaking in that there were no outward signs at home, and he was not visibly ideating in a way that an educator would know to recognize. But certainly his parents' experience highlights the way that a partnership can dissipate or feel abandoned when faced with the highest level of tragedy and loss.

And to the parents reading this book, I hope you see how vital it is to step out of your comfort zone in regards to secrecy, privacy, and shame. It is essential to provide enough information and documentation to the school so that they can adequately support you and your child. While I've encouraged educators to operate with autonomy and grace, they can do this for only so long before requiring more tangible information from a third party, like a doctor, a psychologist, or a treatment provider. This can elevate their ability to fulfill requests for extensions, excusing assignments, or letting a student make something up.

The more information you provide to the school, the more they can do to help you. It's easy to get caught in a cycle where the parents feels frustrated with the school, and the school feels frustrated with the parents. At the end of the day, both parties are really upset about the same thing, which is a lack of information. So we both have to sit at the same table with a shared understanding that with information will hopefully come solutions and advancement in healing.

A CTA for Educators: Who is Your Tow Truck?

As educators, our job is to serve. It's servant leadership, putting the needs of others before our own. Educators work hard and are often exhausted by the amount of themselves—including their personal energy and wellness—that they give to others. During those ten years I spent in the classroom, I would give so much of myself, but at the same time I was living a lie because I wasn't taking care of myself either.

So, there I was serving as a tow truck for others, but who was my tow truck when I broke down? I really had to stop and focus on myself to figure out where within my mental space, my habits, my friendships and other relationships—what was I ignoring? And how was ignoring those factors hindering my ability to provide the highest level of care and education for my students? How was it hindering my ability to authentically collaborate and contribute to the larger school setting as a staff member, a fellow teacher, or a peer to other adults?

As educators, we are diligent about looking out for our students, but we need to adopt that same cadence to the way that we interact with our fellow teachers and educators. Checking in on our colleagues and having tough conversations can feel very uncomfortable. Perhaps you fear overstepping your bounds. But for me, in the very few instances over the course of my career when somebody had the courage to call me out and get me to check my own wellness—although it was uncomfortable, it was always welcomed.

They weren't telling me anything I didn't already know about myself. And their ability to recognize it and approach me from a place of love and support ultimately motivated me to take action. I got the help that I needed to be the best and healthiest version of me.

Levels of Care and the Clinician's Voice

Over the last several years that I have been working in the therapeutic educational space, and more specifically in the last year plus that I have been working in a recovery high school, I really have come to understand the importance of educators listening to the oftentimes unsolicited advice of the clinicians who are providing care.

As educators, we are experts in that domain. And that expertise can sometimes make us become a little bit unteachable ourselves. The clinical voice really encourages us as educators to look past the initial manifestations of student behavior. When the student is acting out or disruptive, unmotivated or isolated, not turning in work, not coming to school—we tend to react with more of an old school traditional punitive consequence. Whereas, longer lasting results will come with trying to seek true understanding of the root causes.

However, as educators, that's not our training. That's not our lane, and we don't need to be in it. But certainly, when we get information from the experts who drive in it every day, we do need to listen. We need to be coachable, and we need to let the information they share dictate our decision-making in the school setting.

Progressive Programs and Partners

In chapter nine, I was only able to focus on a few specific examples of what I refer to as "progressive programs and partners." The truth is that our education system really is stacked with plenty of replicable models of support. These models live within the comprehensive education setting, but they have carved out their own methodology, philosophy, and operating procedures.

It doesn't take a complete overhaul or revolution to slightly change the way that you do business, and in education certainly there's an inundation factor of curricular standards, state standards, national standards, testing, student data, achievement data—all of those markers that can make a school site feel like a pinball going from one task to the other. Collecting one thing, looking at one program, adopting the next. Because of that, with every new program that becomes introduced, I've found that teachers become less motivated to adopt it. They've seen plenty come and go, and they consider this the next trend, or the next fleeting program that won't find its legs.

Although, what I've discovered is that there are plenty of programs that can serve as third party partners. The benefit of a third party partner is that they can serve as outside resources for schools. They can bring in an expert or a curriculum that can help change student culture, or help change teacher perspectives. They can even help educate every stakeholder on the topics of mental health or substance abuse. Specifically, on my website, there are many resources available for educators, parents, and students regionally so that you can find something that might be a good fit for you.

As you conclude reading this book, if I could only have you take one action item away, it would be to conduct a thorough and detailed self-assessment of your own health and wellness, and to lead by example. Now, when I say, "your own health and wellness," that could be you as a person, or as a teacher, counselor, parent, principal or superintendent. We can also scale that "you" to you as a curricular department, or you as a school site, or you as a school district.

What systems do you have in place to support achieving your goals? And where are your blind spots? What are the things within yourself as an individual or an organization that are screaming for your attention but buried under a pile of to-dos, and perhaps even a little bit of denial? So I would start there. Deal with yourself, and lead by example.

Chapter Study

For those of you who would like to further explore the concept that I've outlined in this book, and even take them from the page and into practice at your school— please visit my website and sign up for the book study. The *RECOVER[edu]* book study will take you through each chapter, not only providing a synopsis of the main principles of each chapter, but also providing you with tangibles that will walk you through a reflective process, a professional process, and equip you with tangible tools that you can then easily implement in real time.

As the saying goes, nothing changes if nothing changes. The best time to start is now. While you are operating in a reflective mindset, and engaged with a progressive point of view, take five minutes and go to the website. Register to get more information, tools, updates, emails, and to stay connected.

Contact

If you are interested in collaborating with me at your school or within your district, please reach out! I would love to help you advance your specific goals and needs as a teaching staff, as a leadership staff, or as a school site or district.

To do this, I bring a wealth of information about teenage mental health and recovery from the educators' perspective. Over the course of the last 16 years, I have experienced firsthand almost every layer of the relationship between recovery and education. When speaking to educators, I share my journey through high school and college, into teaching, then becoming assistant principal and traversing my own sobriety and mental health battles. My experience involves a shift from a perpetual phase of survival into one where now I put in the personal work on a daily basis to keep myself well. The attention to that has allowed me to begin to thrive and conquer my professional objectives, as well as my larger goals.

I've been blessed with the unique ability to invite others to take action in their own lives, professions, and work spaces through the anecdotes and humor I share, the vulnerability I deliver, and the authenticity that I wrap every speech, presentation, or workshop in. Please connect with me at www.recoveredu.com or on Instagram: @pattersonperspective. I can't wait to embark on a collaborative and transformative journey with you and your school!

Made in the USA
Coppell, TX
07 May 2020